I0434501

A Brief History of New Caledonia.
From Austronesians to the " destin commun", 1100 BC - 2018 AD.

Frédéric ANGLEVIEL
Professor in Contemporary History,
University of New Caledonia

Translation by Michel PORROT and Max SHEKLETON

@ Editions du GHROC
Groupe de Recherche en Histoire Océanienne
Contemporaine.
Nouméa, 2018.

By the same author

La France des Antipodes. Histoire de la Nouvelle-Calédonie, Ed. Vendémiaire, Paris, 2018, 395 p.

& William Costes, *Art Kanak. Collection William Costes,* Footprint Pacifique, Nouméa, 2018, 128 p.

Histoire illustrée de la Nouvelle-Calédonie, Footprint Pacifique, Nouméa, 2015, 250 p.

Photographies calédoniennes d'antan, Footprint Pacifique, Nouméa, 2017, 210 p.

Un drame de la colonisation. Ouvéa, Nouvelle-Calédonie, mai 1988, Vendémiaire, Paris, 2015, 320 p.

& Yann Bencivengo, *La SLN. 130 ans au service d'une vision industrielle durable,* Ed. SLN-Eramet, Nouméa, 2010, 168 p

& Wadrawane Eddy : *Les Kanak et l'histoire,* les indes savantes, Paris, 2007,

Brève histoire politique de la Nouvelle-Calédonie (1945-2005), éditions GRHOC, Nouméa, 2006, 320 p.

Histoire de la Nouvelle-Calédonie. Nouvelles approches, nouveaux objets, L'Harmattan, Paris, 2006, 350 p.

(dir.) : *La Nouvelle-Calédonie. Terre de métissage,* Annales d'histoire calédonienne, Les indes savantes, Paris, 2004, 274 p.

Les fondements de l'histoire de la Nouvelle-Calédonie. Définition, périodisation, sources, Centre de Documentation Pédagogique, Collection Université, Nouméa, 2004, 201 p.

Historiographie de la Nouvelle-Calédonie ou l'émergence tardive de deux écoles historiques antipodéennes, Publibook, Paris, 2003, 360 p.

(dir.) : *101 mots pour comprendre l'histoire de la Nouvelle-Calédonie,* Ile de Lumière, Nouméa, 1997, 225 p.

& Capecchi Bernard et Douyère Christiane (dir.), *Histoire de la Nouvelle-Calédonie,* CM, CTRDP, Nouméa, 1992.

Introduction

The New Caledonia archipelago, with a people first arrived about three thousand two hundred years ago, is now a French Overseas territory. Throughout the pages, we shall discover the consecutive settlement cycles on la Grande Terre (Main Island) and on the Loyalty Islands, until at the present time.

This approach is resolutely chronological and built around the historic core that is the subject of a reasoned consensus. As an historian for more than thirty years, we incorporated in this book the most recent data, while giving priority to a holistic writing.

Early History, Austronesians settled in several waves. This term includes several origins, all from the Melanesian arc. Some are Lapita potters, others carve petroglyphs, and others bring new yams. Around the year 1000 AD, they become the Kanak. Following the mutual discovery of 1774 by James Cook, adventurers and missionaries get in touch with Melanesians who, then, move on from the age of polished stone and acquire, in a few decades, a new perception of the world.

Recent History, from 1853 to 1945, New Caledonia became a settler colony. This period allows the often controversial Kanak civilization, too long isolated and forgotten, to enter fully into the modern world. This does not happen without excesses, western expansionism feeding itself with the development of tropical raw material.

Currently, New Caledonia is no longer a colony. New Caledonia has been an Overseas Territory from 1946 to 1998, and crossed the period of decolonization through multiple statutory developments. Kanak, as first arrivals, are claiming a greater share in the city. After «Years of Ashes" consecutive to political events, peace is restored in 1988 by the Matignon-

Oudinot Accords. In 1998, with the Noumea Accord, New Caledonia becomes a single entity recognized by the French Constitution

Perspective, New Caledonia will have the possibility to choose its future by a referendum of self-determination which will take place in October 2018. New Caledonians will be able to choose between the current status at the end of the four terms of the Noumea agreement or a new contract bringing New Caledonia close to autonomy or even independence that should have to be built then.

"The past was the time of colonization.
This is the time of sharing, through rebalancing.
The future must be the time of identity in a common destiny ".
Preamble of the Nouméa Acoord, 1998.

First part
The day before yesterday
From the first Austronesian settlement to mutual discovery

Chapter I.
The time before.
3000 years of pre-European history.

Little is known about the early stages of settlement of New Caledonia, due to the absence of any written records. Data from the oral tradition forms a story more or less built, until the arrival of first European explorers, then they etiolate until it disappears completely for the period prior to the fifteenth century AD. Confronting Archaeological data, partial and based on more or less interpretations, remain very fragmented and essentially focused on agricultural techniques, habitat or major features of the diet.

A three-period settlement (-1100 to 1774)
The earliest indisputable traces of human presence in New Caledonia are currently dated around the year 1050 BC; with the arrival of Austronesian populations manufacturing ceramics. These navigators brought with them the art of making original pottery, named Lapita, decorated with many geometric patterns, dotted or incised. Sites discovered to date are located on the coast. Only a few remains of dwellings were found. These are traces of round huts, sometimes surrounded by palisades. Stone ovens were used for cooking, marking the passage, about 200 AD, from roasted meat to boiled food.
Archaeologists have first proposed a periodization based on qualitative evolution of ceramics (Koné period, Naïa-Oundjo period). Today, they prefer the likely evolution of settlement and the progressive complexity of social organization.

First, the ancient prehistoric time or Austronesian time, is an installation phase starting from the coastline, with extensive slash-and-burn cultivation and social organization with undeveloped hierarchy between -1050 and +1000. Undeniably the settlement occurs from west to east in several waves coming from the New Hebrides (Vanuatu) and perhaps sometimes from the Solomon Islands.

Major programs of excavation have led to the discovery of Lapita pottery shards, stone tools or mother pearl (hooks, adzes), bones of endemic animals now extinct (a thirty kilogram megapode, a terrestrial crocodile and horned turtle) and elements of ornamental shells (cowries, cones, giant clams, pearl oysters). At the beginning of the first millennium after Christ, a unique model of pottery in the Pacific appears in Plum: Hemispheric pot with handles. Each region gradually develops its own variations, such as elongated pots, pots with recessed edges or undecorated pots, found mainly in the Loyalty Islands

Engraved petroglyph stones engraved remain a mystery because there is no serious oral tradition relating their history and it has not been yet possible to date them. For its part, Christophe Sand considers that *"their significance goes far beyond land demarcation: competition, initiation ritual, magic, memories, reminders, place of exchange, religious rite, etc."*

Second, the firmly established Melanesian society or the Kanak cultural complex defined by archaeologist Christophe Sand, is the emergence of the great features of the Kanak society that James Cook discovers in 1774. One notes the complete occupation of the land, the presence of intensive agriculture (taro, yam ridges) and the organization of society into small chiefdoms (+1000, -1774). Austronesians, arrived in several waves, are the ancestors of Kanak exactly like the Gauls are the ancestors of the French.

The landscape archaeology demonstrates that the practice of slash-and-burn horticulture, and the one of long fallows led to the disappearance of large trees that kept loamy soils. As written by Christophe Sand, *"These soft soils were quickly washed away during heavy rains or hurricanes, causing landslides and floods of mud, and the enlargement of the plains and estuaries ... The landscape of valleys gradually changed, especially with the significant expansion of some plains."* This phenomenon is the source of immense mangroves areas on the west coast.

The archipelago - which is not yet Caledonian - has become a "full world", conflicts for borders or for control of the best land, cause wars and, in their wake, the construction of fortifications. These monumental buildings have a special importance in the Loyalty Islands where space is more limited. The most impressive site called Hnakudotit on the plateau of the district of La Roche, in Maré. This quadrilateral 180 meters long and 145 m wide includes walls, four meters high and ten meters thick. Initiated in the third century after Christ, it develops along with the conflicts with residents of the close fortification, near Wanunetit.

Third, the late pre-contact period between the fifteenth and the eighteenth centuries, is characterized by the development and individualization of "Kanak countries." Thirty-three languages differentiate the major Melanesian territories.

Networks of alliances and lasting antagonisms appear. A new wave of settlement occurs, the "outliers" - Polynesian migrants sailing from east to west, arrive and settle in the Loyalty Islands and on the East coast of "la Grande Terre".

This is the best documented period because Westerners describe, more or less accurately their respective discoveries. Thus we have first hand descriptions of the latest ceramic tradition, the period of Nera-Oundjo. These potteries are strong and well adapted to the daily cooking. One put some water in a pot, with tubers, crabs or chiken, and the opening was closed by mean of a vegetal plug; then the food was braised. These pots are hand-crafted until the early twentieth century and they go down in history as "marmites kanak" – (kanak pots).

* Snapshot of Kanak society during the first contacts

The pre-European period is known only through excavations, discovery of some objects in shell, bone or stone, but the accounts of early European observers give a relatively accurate picture of the Kanak civilization when it was discovered by the old world and confronted by the existence of the Other.

On the economic front, there is a simple society based on intensive autarkic agriculture and an extensive breeding of hens around the huts. Food supplements are gained by hunting and fishing. No craft or industrial activity differentiated: each one produces what he needs. Round huts and canoes are built together. Therefore there is no city nor real village. Kanak prefer to live in hamlets, huts of members of the same clan radiating from the *"place coutumière"*, (customary square) consisting of a large ceremonial hut and a path lined with columnar pines (male symbol) and coconut palms (female symbol).

Often huts of line Chiefs are built on mounds that reflect the respect they deserve and that protect their inhabitants from humidity. No windows, but a low door which serves as a last protection during wars. Near the central post, a fire remains lit to provide warmth and protection against mosquitoes.

Competition between clans, tribes and between customary areas occupies a prime spot in human relations. For many reasons (breaking of an alliance, conquest of new lands, desecration of taboo places...), groups are frequently at war. The *"kanak currency"* (la monnaie Kanak) is circulated in order to warn allies, ancestors are invoked for their protection, weapons are prepared: spears, slings, clubs... The fights, which are often only ambushes and skirmishes, give rise to the practice of ritual cannibalism.

There is division of labour. For instance, during the construction of the huts, the men cut down the tree trunks, build the frame; women fetch straw for the roofs, weave mats for the interior. Children go naked. Adults are topless and have on their body many ornaments of pearl or polished stone. Women are dressed in a very tight and long skirt belt made of bourao. The men wear a penis sheath called the bagayou. To protect themselves from rain or cold, men and women may don capes made of vegetable fibers.

Cultivation of yam and taro occupies most of the time: men clear the land, plough the soil, prepare the irrigation channels for taro, harvest early yams, while women break the clods, plant and beautify the fields. This peasant society experiences frequent food shortages: lean periods, ravages of hurricanes, withering crops due to drought or bushfires. The geographer Jean-Pierre Doumenge notes that *"traditional society was a world of survival. Eating well was the highest form of welfare.
"*

* An idealized time before

Today, some observers believe that the time before was the golden age of Kanak civilization. Their considerations take into account the tragedies of colonization, while hiding the internal problems crossing the pre-European Kanak countries. All chroniclers of the first contacts evoke the very low status of the Melanesian woman, who was responsible for all the harshest and most repetitive work. All descriptions show that traditional society was based on an economy of scarcity and that malnutrition and deaths were frequent during famines. Wars were not destructive in terms of loss of life, but were frequent and responsible for of famines resulting from crop destruction.

Kanak cannibalism remains a hidden reality. It is not time to conclude on such a subject that requires a lot of research and studies, but we can assert at least three points. First, cannibalism has been a kanak practice during the pre-european period and protohistorical times.

Second, it was primarily a warrior ritual, with few drifts feared and criticized by Melanesians themselves, linked to the shortage of animal proteins;

Third, the Europeans developed, during the progressive colonization of the island, a very exaggerated and demeaning discourse on cannibalism, even though it disappeared in the 1860s as an acceptable social practice. This paradox is related to the changing relationships between the two communities, the colonizers needing to evoke the "savagery" of the Melanesians when these are unilaterally deprived of their freedom by the colonized status.

*A marquetry of small chiefdoms

With regard to the social and religious organization, trades occurs during traditional ceremonies and are intended to create, reinforce or perpetuate alliances between the different clans, on the occasion of weddings, adoptions or births. Exchanges are always equivalent: it is the gift and the reciprocal gifts.

The chief governs major traditional ceremonies, such as the feast of yams, mourning, weddings and burials. Few external signs differentiate the chief or elder brother, from the rest of the group. Arbitrating conflicts of traditions and land disputes, he is the guarantor of tradition, of the great moral and social values of the Kanak society. Relationships exist between small and large leaderships and between valleys. Customary paths help maintain alliances with donations of ceremonial objects such as adzes, greenstone axes and Kanak currencies.

Like everywhere in the world, groups develop conquest strategies. This phenomenon is more visible in the Loyalty Islands where Polynesian influence and geography give greater weight to large leaderships. A small human group coming from southern Vanuatu, the Xetriwaan, appropriates, by war and marriages, leading positions both in Lifou and in the Loyalty Islands or in the south of La Grande Terre. Because of the absence of major invasive migrations coming from the Melanesian arc during centuries, each entity, specific by his language or his spatial unity, becomes a "Kanak country," that is to say, an isolate in competition with the neighbouring valleys

Long, anthropologists have considered, like Pastor Maurice Leenhardt, that leaders listened to the advice of the elders and that they were men of peace and mediation. Alban Bensa revisited this issue by integrating the evolutionary element, that is to say History, to previous partial analyzes. It appears that the Kanak leader of the first half of the nineteenth century is a warrior, or at least he is seconded by warlords. He and his clans are regularly in conflict with neighbouring groups.

The first contacts develop warlike practices, allowing the most bellicose leaders like Gondou on the west coast, to acquire firearms and iron axes. Finally, the colonial administration imposes a kind of *pax romana* to "native" chiefs. Pacification is part of the civilizing mission and secures the front of settlers who first reach the western plains, and later on the eastern valleys. From then on the Kanak leader gradually loses his warlike character and becomes the big brother full of wisdom described by Mr. Leenhardt.

The gods are the founding ancestors of clans. The spirits are those of the deceased. After their death, their successors invoke them to encourage rainfall, crops grow, and to obtain their protection during wars ... Usually their skulls rest on a rock arranged for this purpose and this is where the invocations are made. On arrival of Westerners, the bodies of the dead were often deposited on the ground in the forest, so that the flesh leaves the bones which were then piously collected. The introduction of dogs and pigs, during the passage of James Cook in 1774 radically transformed the practice. To avoid desecration of bodies, some placed their dead in the roots of banyan tree, and later others used wooden sarcophagi to honour some paramount chiefs.

There is no clergy but witches, or takata, who possess magical objects, who have the support of totemic forces and know the beneficial or destructive effects of some medicinal plants. Each clan is protected by a totem and respects the animals or plants concerned. There is no polytheistic pantheon like in Polynesia. The lack of territorial unit probably explains the lack of common myths in the whole archipelago.

The most obvious "pagan" practices disappeared with Christianization, but uses concerning popular culture and respect of meteorological calendar, have mostly lasted until today. Thus Emma Hadfield notes in 1920 that uses, in Lifou, imposes that nobody mentions plantations of relatives, otherwise they perish. Similarly, no one should point at young shoots, unless they run the risk to rot.

Jean-Marie Tjibaou wrote in 1981: *"It must be said that we went from the Stone Age to the moon rockets in the space of a hundred years, while it took a long time to Europe to do the same. How long ago did you leave the Stone Age? And since the advent of the industrial world, everything goes faster and faster."*

And he added in 1985: *"Return to tradition is a myth; I am trying to say and repeat it. This is a myth. No nation ever experienced it. The search for identity, the model, for me it is ahead, never back. This is an ongoing reformulation. And I would say that our current struggle is to be able to include, as much as possible, elements from our past, our culture, in the building of the model of man and of society we want to build the city. Some may have other analysis, but this is my way of seeing. Our identity is before us. Finally, when we are dead, people will take our image, will put it in niches and it will serve them to build their own identity. Otherwise, we are never able to kill the father, we are done for."*

Chapter 2.
Early history and drama of the microbial shock (1774-1853)

Protohistory consists in grouping the period of mutual discovery and the time of first contacts, instead of the traditional approach that distinguishes them. Indeed, the classical period of "the discovery of the Pacific" had the effect, firstly, to give the impression that emerged lands were unknown by humanity before the arrival of Westerners and, secondly, to minimize the role played by indigenous peoples in the discovery of the other

The native appeared as an object, and not as an actor.

However, the three hundred years long story about a few hundred sailors appeared exaggerated in comparison with the study of changes, both in cosmogony and demography, driven by the emergence of difference and Western "modernity" in a island environment populated by between 60 000 and 100 000 Melanesians.

In fact, it was not before the late installation of the first beachcombers and that of the first missionaries that real human relationships appear. Yet the life of Kanaks will be transformed by these coastal intrusions: technical revolutions (iron, firearms, glass, fabrics), introduction of new animal species (dogs, pigs, and goats and cattle), cosmogonic shocks (Europeans as pale as the ancestors, Christian missionaries), and especially microbial shock (long isolated, unknown pathologies in Oceania)

Demographically, this microbial shock resulted in the death of 40 to 80% of the initial population, and led to a serious economic and political crisis prior to colonization. In some regions, there is a shortage of labour for the taro fields. In other valleys, the collapse of the social organization of Kanak countries prevents the mobilization of workers.

Few researchers have attempted to address this problem which is based as well on the upheavals associated with the use of new objects, simple and fundamental like metal or glass, as on the integration, in a cyclical thought; of a new model incorporating the concepts of evolution and social, economic, political, or religious progress.

* Late opening to the world (1774 - 1840)

During his second voyage to the Pacific, after exploring south of the New Hebrides archipelago (Vanuatu), British captain James Cook sails to New Zealand, when midshipman Colnett shots a new land. It was September 4th 1774. J. Cook calls this island New Caledonia.

He stays in Balade from the 4 to the 13 September. He gives local chiefs many objects unknown to the Kanak. He distributes seeds, a couple of dogs and a couple of pigs. The first soon form bands that attack chicken of the tribes and local fauna. Pigs, returned to wildlife, colonize the central island. Then James Cook sails southward along the east coast.

On September 23, 1774, he is in sight of Kunié Island which he names Isle of Pines because of the numerous Araucarias (columnar pines). After him comes La Perouse who explores the west coast of New-Caledonia in 1789. His ships wreck in Vanikoro (Solomon Islands), all sailors perished in this wreckage. So we will never know what contacts this explorer was able to establish with the Kanaks.

In search of the unfortunate La Perouse, Bruni d'Entrecasteaux sails the Caledonian waters in 1792 and 1793.He names many maritime places (Huon, Surprise, Beautemps-Beaupré ...) and draws the first chart of the west Coast.

Upon initial contact, James Cook considers that the Kanak are friendly and honest people, who live a peaceful life in comfort. On the contrary, Bruni d'Entrecasteaux thinks they are malnourished, aggressive and thieves. It seems that the situation has changed in the area between 1774 and 1793. Some believe that this change is due to the arrival of new groups of people in the Balade-Pouébo vicinity. Others believe that a natural disaster would explain the Kanak change of behavior. Still, others believe that James Cook unimaginable gifts would have led, for their possession, to conflicts between all the tribes of the far North.

If the ships of the Australian colonies, going to Asia, often sail through the so called channel of the Loyalty Islands, these islands are very roughly represented on the maps of the early nineteenth century. Dumont d'Urville rediscovers Maré, Lifou and Ouvea in 1827. During a second voyage to the Pacific in 1840, he establishes the definitive map of the Loyalty Islands.

Usually French and British "discoverers" warships stay a few days or a few hours at anchor. Relations remain very superficial and descriptions, as well as drawings and engravings, provide little information about the realities of Kanak countries.

* The pre-colonial time of adventurers (1820 - 1860)

From the early nineteenth century, whalers and sperm whales hunters discover rich in cetaceans South Seas. They go to New Caledonian waters from 1820s. Boats drop anchor in the Loyalty Islands and in the north of New Caledonia to stock up on food and water. A station for the extraction of whale oil even operates in Lifou. But replacing whale-oil by fuel and depletion of whale herds lead to the end of this activity in New Caledonia after 1860.

Á the same time, the development of the first Australian centres contributes to the establishment of trade routes in the Pacific and soon allows making big profits on foodstuffs. The opening of the Chinese market, big producers of tea but having little interest in European manufactured products, allows merchants to get paid in sandalwood (fragrant wood) and trepang (sea cucumber) at the highest price. It is therefore noted the appearance of a triangular trade based on navigation from Australia to the Pacific Islands and from Oceania to China and finally from Asia to Australian ports.

The trade of sandalwood causes the early trade between the Melanesians of New Caledonia and the modern European world. These relationships - sometimes turbulent - last from its discovery in 1840 until the late 1850s.

From 1840, the first Europeans settle in New Caledonia. Caledonian coasts progressively receive *"beachcombers"*, that is to say «beach scouring people," westerners: shipwrecked, deserters or mutineers who escaped the wrath of ocean. History has lost the surnames of the first generation, especially Anglo-Saxon, arrived before colonization. It remembers the names of their successors (Streeter, Forest, Young, Winchester, etc.), because they have been bridges between civilizations.

Then, ship-owners Robert Townes and James Paddon build permanent stations in order to collect trade products, the first two in the Isle of Pines in 1848, the next in Nou Island in 1854. Sometimes they also settle some sailors ashore to create temporary trading posts. These agents are exchanging items of iron, fabric, glass beads, tobacco, pipes, and soon a few rifles and bullets against sandalwood and voluntary work of Melanesians (cutting, cleaning and transporting timber to the beach).Traders also show interest by in products like mother-of-pearl, coconut oil and sea cucumbers

Trepang fishermen (or bêche de mer) have an important role during this period of first contacts, because they stay several months ashore among the tribes and their activity requires protection and active participation of Kanaks

French and English warships began to cruise in New Caledonian waters. Some come for scientific studies. Others are ordered to study the economic potential and estimate the power of the local authorities. Others again are responsible for taking possession of land considered vacant according to international law established by the European continent. Thus the reports made by officers of *Alcmene*, following a trip to New Caledonia in 1851, appear to favour taking possession by the French Empire.

* **Time of missionary settlements (1840-1851)**

English missionaries of the London Missionary Society (LMS) decide, from 1797 to Christianize the Pacific. The New Caledonian archipelago is achieved by 1840. Protestant missions are based on few courageous Oceanian ministers, *the teachers*, coming from Samoa or Rarotonga. Their first attempts are unsuccessful on La Grande Terre and in the Isle of Pines.

The Kanak society is still much closed. Thus the *teacher* Taunga, the only Polynesian evangelist who left a pre-colonial testimony written in Touaourou: *"Paganism was diminishing but still the majority of the population did not even wear clothes. They were still pagans. In 1845 the missionary ship* John Williams *arrived and Noe and I went on board. The two missionaries were very worried about our fate because of the bad intentions of the population and continual threats of death that were addressed to us. They told us to accompany them on board the ship. A ship's captain who had anchored at the Isle of Pines told us (stated they) that the people of this island intended to declare war to our island and that you will be both killed during the month of May"*.

The *teachers* suffer conflicts between chiefdoms and Europeans. The Paramount Chief of the Isle of Pines realizes that epidemics are increasing with the arrival of sandalwood traders. He blames the God of the whites for that. He also finds that his family members are mistreated by sailors without the *teachers* intervening between them. He then sends the *teachers* away. Unfortunately, because of technical issues, their ship returns to the Isle of Pines. The crew of *the Star* and the *teachers* are massacred in 1842, ending the first attempt of Protestant evangelization in South of New-Caledonia.

British missionaries then turn to the Loyalty Islands. Conversion of Chiefs Nidoish Naisseline in Maré (1848), and Bula in Lifou (1851), allows *teachers* Tataïo and Fao to settle permanently. Later, European ministers settled and Ouvea is reached in 1856.

This success, the largest obtained in Melanesia, explains why the Loyalty Islands still have a large majority of Protestants today and why many traditions remain alive (religious, culinary and sociological, words of English origin in the islands languages, cricket ...).

Because of its particular church organization, the Protestant Church gladly recognized the essential role of Melanesian notables and the importance of their free will in the acceptance and diffusion of Protestantism. Kerry Howe has developed this approach, rightly considering that "progress of acculturation does not necessarily result in any form of social dislocation."

The first conversions of Oceanians to Protestant faith encourage priests of the Society of Mary to set up in Melanesia. At the end of 1843 a French warship, the *Bucéphale*, brings Bishop Guillaume Douarre and four Marist missionaries to Balade, coming from Wallis. They develop a pragmatic *"science of mission"* and become the first linguists and early ethnographers of the archipelago.

These men in cassocks, like ministers in three piece suits condemn cannibalism and they regret that women is overworked with work. They struggle against polygamy or the custom of abandoning the sick or elderly. In 1845, Father Rougeyron writes: *"Caledonian women need religion to free them, as elsewhere, from their state of slavery. They grovel to the feet of man, like beasts of burden. It is up to them to bear burdens, to cook, to fetch some food and take care of the fields when land is cleaned. They have the largest share in the works, and the smallest in the sweetness of household. Is there a good bite to eat, immediately the chef puts a taboo on it. The woman can watch her husband eating, but she cannot take part, otherwise she would die.*

Is she sick? Immediately she is locked away, at night she sleeps outside or under some branches more or less intertwined. She must remain there, exposed to rain and injuries of the air. And the unfortunate must stay apart when she has her period; she is forbidden then to live with her husband. Is she disobedient, unfaithful? Her enraged husband treats her with an unequalled barbarity, he breaks her skull with a rock. And then comes the surgeon who, with his shells, tears the surrounding flesh of the wound. That is enough to thrill the hardest heart»

The following year, he reports his ancient prejudices: *"I had imagined that savage people live in the woods, like ferocious beasts, and that each of them live in his shelter without any social contacts. Alas, how wrong I was! These men are perfectly similar to us, with a few differences that are not essential. They live in a society. Their huts are not built in forests but in the plains or valleys ... they are less stubborn than some good people that we find in our mountain villages. They are simple, it is true, but they have never seen anything else than what exist in their islands.*

In 1847 new epidemics and drought occur. It follows wars and robberies. Kanak, not only provide more food to the missionaries, but they attack in July, the mission in Balade provided with supplies. Brother Blaise Marmoiton suffers martyrdom. After years of exile, the Marist missionaries settled in the Isle of Pines in 1848, then return to Balade in 1851.

Then comes the time of mission stations, the settlement of which results, during the period 1850-1880, in the conversion of more than half of the Kanaks of La Grande Terre. The Marists, following the main "customary paths", on the east coast, and later on the west coast, regularly increase their progress while facing the problem of "blocking third".

Indeed, the traditional opponents of the new converts prefer to stay "pagans." Secondly, missionaries have to face the clash of cultures, misunderstandings are legion. Father Fabre while translating a catechism into *drehu* notes in 1867: *"Translating with clarity and precision our Catholic teaching into indigenous language and thereby putting it within reach of the intelligence of Oceanian populations is not easy to do. Sometimes it is the term of the original that has no counterpart*

19

in the native language; sometimes it is the French turn of the phrase that refuses to bow to the turn of the islanders' language». Taking possession of New Caledonia by France, a predominantly Catholic country, explains that only Catholic missionaries are allowed; throughout the nineteenth century, to settle on the mainland. That is why, even today, this land is mainly Catholic.

The conversion has been a voluntary and deliberate choice of the Kanaks. Missionaries of the two major Christian Churches have helped them, grouping together villages away from traditional places of worship, educating boys and girls and becoming linguists and ethnographers, to facilitate the dissemination of their religious message.

* A real trading period
As elsewhere in the Pacific, this protohistoric period is a true period of trade and exchange, where Western adventurers were working for their personal interests, while forcing themselves, more or less gracefully, to respect local customs.

Some modern historians consider that the terms of first exchanges were unbalanced. For them, buying large quantities of food or commercial products, against few objects of trafficking, was a reprehensible practice. Thus they do a misinterpretation of history.

First, venture into the Pacific Ocean was still very dangerous and never sailors would have ventured in such long and hazardous voyages, if the benefits were not important. Second, any international trade is based on the purchase of products readily available locally, and at a moderate price, against products sought by the natives, what gives them a high added value. Third, Kanaks, before the arrival of Europeans, did not know glass, metal, pets other than chicken, or tissues except tapa, what logically gave a great value to these products that they could not manufacture under no circumstances,

Part two
Yesterday
A conflictual colonial period (1853-1945)

Chapter III
The "small Southern France"
Second French colonial settlement

The colonial period is the period during which the legal status of colony of the French Colonial Empire was applied to New Caledonia, between taking possession in 1853 and its accession to the status of Overseas Territory in 1946. There has been no colonial war in the taking possession, as the Kanak society had no state organization, and his very basic level of technology prompted it to welcome this new wave of migration. The incidents begin when the French State, which has taken unilaterally possession of all the land in 1855, develops the land colonization of La Grande Terre.

New Caledonia was a special colony in the sense that it was a convict settlement, but more because it was one of the only two settlement colonies of France, the other being Algeria. This period corresponds to the European expansion, with its shadows and lights, at a time when the relations of domination were excessive everywhere: whether between bosses and labour, who were forbidden to join a union; between husbands and their wives who were legally minor; between pioneers and colonized peoples who lost their sovereignty and most of their land.

And indeed, much of the modern history of New Caledonia must be read through the prism of the subordination of the interests of the Kanak country to the interest of pioneers' frontier, and to those of the penal administration during the colonial period. Meanwhile, New Caledonia is characterised by the establishment of ticket of leave prisoners and of recruited labourers coming from New Hebrides, Bourbon Island or Asia. These "involuntary settlers" and those "victims of history", far from being pioneer conquerors, participated at the time by their sweat and pain, to the construction of today's New Caledonia.

In another sense, Tjibaou notes during an interview in May 1985: *"When the Romans invaded Gaul, I think that is what led to the emergence of consciousness of Gaul. It is a bit like home. ... There was never a nationalist claim, as long as there is no nation that alienates the sovereignty of another nation. "*

* Settlement colonization and the first Kanak revolt

The government of Napoleon III seeks a new land, free from any European occupation in order to establish a penal colony. In addition, France wants to strengthen its presence in the Pacific, still weak, while England already possesses Australia and New Zealand and plans to annex New Caledonia. And finally Catholic missionaries and French trade vessels "must" be protected and supported.

Rear-Admiral Febvrier Despointes, coming from Tahiti, organizes in Balade on 24, September 1853 the official ceremony of annexation in the presence of missionaries and local leaders. The ceremony is repeated at the Isle of Pines, September 29, in the presence of the High Chief Vendegou who signs the official document. Febvrier Despointes dies of illness on board the *Catinat* during his trip return to Tahiti.

It should be noted that Captain Tardy Montravel arrives on January 5, 1854 at the Isle of Pines. On January 9, he is put in charge of this colony, administratively attached (until 1860) to the French Establishments of Oceania. Rereading the ministerial instructions, he notes that if the possession was held, as desired, in two *"positions permitting to stay there permanently and to fortify the position"*, its predecessor did not have the necessary health to follow the letter the same instructions.

Thus, from January 23, he makes the Chief of the tribe of Poum to sign a statement confirming the possession of New Caledonia. With the return of summer, Tardy de Montravel starts to sail along the east coast and then along the west coast, meeting the leaders, informing them of the possession and persuading them to swear allegiance to France. On May 7, Big Chief Bouarate signs for the region of Hienghène. Then it was the turn of the Chiefs Boula Kouaoua and Kai Canala. After June 23, 1854, the French flag is hoisted in a bay that will be Noumea, Tardy Montravel gets the homage of Chief Quindo (or Kuindo) August 16

The various documents, once they reach Paris, are validated by the Emperor and it is on February 13, 1854, that the Imperial Monitor announced to the French the creation of the new colony. Later, the English missionaries of the LMS denying that the Loyalty Islands are part of the dependencies of New Caledonia, Governor Charles Guillain goes there and makes a second annexation in June 1864, for Maré and Lifou. A similar ceremony was held in June 1865 in Ouvea.

From 1853 to 1860, New Caledonia is attached to the French Establishments in Oceania (Tahiti). The new colony needs an administrative centre. Tardy de Montravel finally chooses the site of Noumea which offers many advantages. The harbour is wide, deep and well sheltered from the wind. The site is also easy to defend. In 1854, the name of Port-de-France is given to the first New Caledonian town. In order to defend the site, a fort, Fort Constantine is quickly built. The first urban lots are allocated and also the first rural concessions around the capital.

In 1855, the extension of colonization causes opposition of some Kanak leaders due to a slow but steady land dispossession. On the east coast, the insurgents are mainly chiefs Bouarate (Hienghène) and Bouéone (Balade). In the region of Port-de-France, the opposition is led by Chief Kuindo. The Administration authorizes the Marist mission to open two reductions in La Conception (1855) and St. Louis

(1856). These institutions gather Catholic Kanak of this area and many groups, essentially coming from the East Coast. This true "glaze" is repeatedly attacked by the tribes of the Great South who refuse to give up part of their land for settlement.

These early revolts occur without any coordination, and they are suppressed one after the other. Governor Joseph du Bouzet justifies the pacification of the south-west of La Grande Terre in his farewell speech in 1858: *"Indigenous (...) today understand that their interest is to live in peace with us, and that we came not to bring them war, but the benefits of our religion and our civilization. "*

From 1862 New Caledonia is actually built as a separate colony. Everything is done from the perspective of the imperial administration: organizing transportation, penal settlement, free colonization. The first governor, Charles Guillain must also create the administration, organize the economy and lead an indigenous policy. He promotes agriculture and livestock through, among other things, a model farm installed in Yahoué, while engineer Jules Garnier explores, the mineral wealth of La Grande Terre from 1863 to 1866. In 1866, the name of the capital changes. The *Moniteur Impérial* states: *"Port-de-France is no more ... Long live Noumea."*

The complexity of the relations of colonization appears when Jules Garnier invited the "village chief of Poimbey" for dinner: *"The face of the old man, still serious, anxious even, therefore took a more confident expression. However, he was with his most hated enemies, with those who sought to remove its independence, to him the old Savage, that is to say, the freest man and the most jealous of his freedom; but the meal was good, and the Indians themselves are graceful with those who treat them well. "*

Jules Garnier shows, in 1862, the contradiction, today obvious, between a colonial discourse, which is adorned with humanistic ideals and civilizing, and a colonial reality by nature spoliatory. *"One consequence of these indigenous revolts is that, right after, all their land is immediately seized to install settlers. Also, from a certain point of view, pretty weird though, it is lucky that the natives occasionally go off on jaunts because their land, immediately confiscated, soon increases the public wealth and serves the settlers; otherwise one would have to act with more brutality and – it must be said - more frankness, in driving them back to their mountains, as the British did in Australia, in Van Diemen, etc. The colonizing and human theory, which calls for its extension among these people by a gradual mixing of the conquering race and the conquered race, here is unworkable, because the native and the white, with a natural instinct, repel and cannot agree on any point. It is certain that the Kanak like all savages, live miserably on a land that would feed abundantly a number of European inhabitants fifty times larger (we have seen that this colony could receive two million inhabitants, while the native population is barely thirty thousand); Isn't it fair that they give way to those who, by patient and active study, were able for many centuries passed, to gather all the knowledge and materials that allow them to achieve this wonderful result to take from the soil fifty times more than the savages can do, and isn't it a law assented to every moment in nature by thousands of facts that the skilful pushes back the clumsy, and the powerful pushes back the weak "*

Charles Guillain, a convinced Saint-Simonian, is a strong supporter of both the assimilation and colonization. Assimilation - from the perspective of the colonizer - must promote peaceful and tolerant meeting of the two cultures. In 1867, the tribes are created and the following year, tribal lands are organised as "reservations" and declared "inalienable and unsalable". The reservations allow to free the lands for the benefit of the pioneers of free colonization and later for the penal colonization, while protecting the traditional society from the excesses of that dual colonization.

By encouraging small property, that is to say, the sale of concessions ranging from 5 to 500 ha, Guillain attracts some immigrants, but distance vis-à-vis France remains an obstacle to any real movement of European immigration. In 1870, there were 1,300 Europeans settled in Noumea, Mount Dore and St. Vincent

Noumea remains a garrison town with all that entails: taverns, gambling dens, brothels with Australian or New Hebridean women. The opening and development of the prison accentuate the dangerousness of the city, where fighting between Pacific Islanders, among sailors, soldiers, adventurers and released prisoners, are common.

From 1855, an Advisory Board of Directors is established by Governor du Bouzet (of EFO) to advise him locally. It becomes the Privy Council in 1874. It includes the Governor, the four chiefs of service of the time, the military commander and two colonial advisers chosen among notables.

The different services are created as needed and, as noted by Pierre Gascher, they had no specific remits: *"We always added to the building without subtracting anything and as the Prison Administration complicated everything, all became disparate"*.

The decree of December 12, 1874 determines the organization of the government of the island. The Governor is the commander-in-chief and responsible for the high administration of New Caledonia. He represents the authority of the Head of State, and not that of the Minister of Marine, which is a special provision. He exercises the military power, alone and indivisibly. It is true that all the governors until 1884 are naval officers.

He promulgates the laws that must receive their application in the island but only the Head of State decides what acts can be applied. So we pass from the unit of authority tempered by the exercise of local liberties, a practice relating to the assimilation theory, to the principle of special legislation that allows some segregation between free settlers, released prisoners, enlisted soldiers, transported convicts and

26

indigenous. Originally, very few colonial officials allow law enforcement in the interior of the main island and the Loyalty Islands. After the insurrection of 1878, New Caledonia is divided, the following year, into five districts defined in terms of technical considerations: their areas had to be almost identical. The Department says in 1885: *"The role of the district chief is before all a protective role, he must ensure that, in the territory he administers, no injustice can be committed to the detriment of indigenous"*.

The colonial administration does not favour the democratization of institutions. It is forced to accept gradually the intervention of local notables because New Caledonia is a settlement colony. Governor Saisset sets up, in 1859, a local council of twelve members appointed by the Governor for a period of three years. From its second session, February 9, 1860, Mayor Victor Coudelou and counsellors note that responsibilities are granted to them by the military authorities, but no revenue allows to consider the establishment of a municipal policy except creating taxes that would be very unpopular in the small civilian community of which they are the most influential members. The City Council turns to its creator and urges the establishment of a specific budget taken from the general budget of the colony. Accordingly, Commander Durand chooses to dissolve the first City Council July 21, 1860.

A new Council is finally appointed and established in 1874. The administration sees it as a simple room for registration of its decisions related to the development of the perimeter of the municipality. Regularly, some advisers come into conflict with the aims of the governor and his administration. They are then simply removed from office and replaced by more complacent Noumeans, who are chosen from "supplementary lists".

Finally, the Third Republic accedes to the wishes of the population of Noumea. The Governor therefore promulgates on March 8, 1879, the organization of real municipal institutions for the municipality of Noumea. The first elections are held in 1879, the mayor and his two assistants are designated by the Governor. So communal freedom is still relative. From 1882 the mayor is elected by the counsellors. It should be noted that the City Council will long remain a training ground and an anteroom for candidates for election to the General Council, which is established in 1885. Municipal competences remain very limited. The mayor therefore often uses the vote to communicate his wishes, both to the governors and the citizens. Thus, on August 27, 1888 the Council approves the following wish: *"considering that it is well known that during the stay, in the port of Noumea, of ships coming from outside, a very large quantity of goods are unloaded and put for sale without first paying custom duties .... wishes to place an employee on board any vessel coming from outside to prevent the landing of goods undeclared to the customs."*

Municipal committees are created in 1879 in the main centres of colonization to initiate the settlers of the "bush" in the handling of their affairs. They stagnate because of the small number of qualified candidates. Indeed, the settlers, scattered over a wide area and busy with their various agricultural efforts, ignore the public affairs.

A General Council is finally established in 1885. The sixteen representatives elected in the first mandate are MM. Dézarnaulds, Président, Violet, Delabaume, Simon Tauveron, Brown, Bouscarel, De Greslan, Evain, Maurin, Escande Pezron, Leconte, Revercé, Pelatan and Servet. It should be noted that the mandate is free and compensations to facilitate the election of small settlers will have to wait for the twentieth century

The competences of the General Council are limited by its founding decree that authorizes the Governor to suspend or dissolve it "by order made by the private Council." Gradually, through the annual vote of the colonial budget, the General Council increases its influence in social and economic domains. It should be noted that Article 46 stipulates: «Any *political wish is forbidden."* Normally, Councillors flatter their electorate, deploring the real or imagined abuses of administrative offices. New Caledonian settlers resent being treated as second class citizens, typical bitterness among colonial settlements. At the same time, they intuitively know that the sustainability of their settlement is based on the protection the highest interests of the State and on the army of the Republic.

All historians agree to estimate that New Caledonia was a colony without settlers, and we might add, without workers of colonization. Indeed, if we must refute the myth that the indigenous population was, from the beginning, reluctant to work for newcomers, traders, soldiers and settlers, it is evident that, by the 1860s, most of the Kanak refuse to work for those who dispossess them of their lands or for those who offered insufficient salaries. Moreover, Kanak, as warriors out of any market economy, and also as men in charge of large agricultural labour, had neither desire nor always time to work for the developing colonization. They avoided, as much as possible, any farm work, low paid and considered degrading.

The most inquisitive preferred to go to Noumea, the only real urban centre of the island, to discover modernity. Some Melanesians then become porters, native policemen, or office workers. One of them is even in the 1860s, a teacher-instructor in Noumea.

Therefore were always Kanak ready to work with the various agents of colonization, but their number proves increasingly inadequate while needs increase. On the one hand, they lived poorly their subjection formalized by the decree of January 1863, which had created the temporary and paid engagement of 150 Kanaks per year, and especially the act of May 6, 1871, which stipulated that every indigenous male 18 to 25 years would be called to work for the administration for one year. All the men had a chore of 5 working days per year. These benefits in kind partly explain the various rebellions of 1860-1870. On the other hand, we see throughout the nineteenth century a population decline. This leads settlers to seek outside of the colony, too sparsely populated, the labour they lack.

By 1865, a man named Austin fetched 33 New Hebrideans. He sells them, or rather he sells to interested New Caledonian settlers for just the cost of the trip. The same year. Mr. Henry, a settler from the New Hebrides, enters into an agreement with the governor of New Caledonia that specifies that, in return for the supply of 100 New Hebridean for a lump sum of 2500 F, paid by the Treasury, he will get a monopoly of sandalwood trading in the north of the mainland for three years. These Oceanians are recruited for one year and the administration is in charge of their return. Henry continues this practice several years connected with the settlers, and even when, in 1867, he doubles the price of research and transport of this human cargo, the colonial administration covers this real slave trade, satisfying itself in 1869 with imposing a medical examination to ensure the health of immigrants. When, in 1869, John Higginson takes over from Henry, he obtains the increase in the price per head at 75 F, justifying this increase by the "unfair" competition of the markets in Australia and Fiji.

The decree of March 26, 1874 stipulates: *"... the conditions for the introduction of Asian, African and Ocenian workers and the conditions of their protection in the colony."* This decree creates, among other things, the Immigration Department, says that entry can be made only in the port of Noumea and organizes a three-day quarantine after which immigrants are registered and entrusted to their employers. They owe housing and clothing to their employees, a detailed food ration, medical care, repatriation and burial costs, if any. The enlisted must work twelve hours in summer and eleven in the cool season. If he makes a mistake or deserts he is punishable of discipline workshop.

The 200 to 500 New Hebrideans who work permanently in Noumea, since 1856, come under this new law that, if it channels and normalizes their immigration, does not prevent its development, necessitated by the economic expansion of the colony. The colony still misses workers, they work as servants or employees in Noumea, or as farm labour and miners.

From 1880 they are still more than 2000 in the colony until the end of the nineteenth century. A petition in 1882, in favour of keeping this immigration more or less forced, is very explicit about the position of employers: *"They are naturally calm, docile, fundamentally honest and industrious enough, especially when compared to the Kanaks of New Caledonia and Loyalty Islands. For us they are a kind of natural gendarmerie. "*

More than 14,000 New Hebrideans live in New Caledonia in the nineteenth century, this generic term including some Solomon Islanders, approximately 10% of the total. Half of them die on the spot, a high mortality rate of 5 to 10% per year due to poor living conditions: poor housing, undiversified and often doctored "official" rations, painful or dangerous work. Those who escape are usually caught by the indigenous Kanak police. Young people aged 18 to 24 are the most sought after labour. There is a special demand for women and young children. In a society with a highly unbalanced sex ratio in favour of men, New Hebridean women are sought as concubines.

Another feature of the traffic is the high proportion of very young recruits. In the early years the legal age was set at 6 years and it increased in 1893 to the age of 9 and to 10 years in 1904. The reason for the introduction of these children, who represent 40% of certain contingents, is due to a regulatory provision allowing employees to keep these children until they reach adulthood. This practice strongly suggests slavery by his contempt for the individual and its commodification. It is not surprising that a friend of Victor Schoelcher informed him of this practice in 1880, in order to forbid it.

This very laborious population progressively settles down; these workers would primarily return home with a rifle and other trade goods. Moreover, it was said in the islands, *"No good Noumea, Noumea no pay"*.

* The penal colony in "La Nouvelle"

In 1863 New Caledonia is designated as a penal colony for convicts to hard labour, also called "les forçats" or "les transportés", or more commonly, "les bagnards". The first 250 arrived in 1864 aboard the *Iphigenia*: they are obliged to build their own cells. They will be more than 20 000 men and 250 women.

The government of Napoleon III wants to permanently remove unwanted persons and also give them a chance for rehabilitation; the incorrigible are send to French Guyana. The 1854 law is based on the notion of rehabilitation before the time: *"The convicts who will be worthy of indulgence made by their conduct, their work and their repentance will be granted a concession of land."*

The first governor, Charles Guillain is the champion of these strong and humanist politics. In his speech welcoming the second convoy of convicted workers in 1866, he said: *"In our human, but always perfectible societies, the most brilliant individuals may have moments of failure, without being condemned forever. Whatever criminal may have been your past, I want to believe that your souls are not fully closed with noble aspirations, that your hearts still vibrate to the idea of family life, to the prospect of a social life reconquered by an irreproachable conduct now »*.

The objective of the criminal settlement was to officially populate the colony of New Caledonia and "regenerate" the condemned. From 1869, the administration instituted ticket of leave convicts, to whom it assigns land between four and five acres that they must develop in order to finally get the full ownership. They must therefore be rehabilitated through work, the objective being to create in valley after valley, colonies of peasants.

It was the great plan of governor Guillain. The concessions were originally granted to the best subjects, but only at the end of their sentence. From 1878 access to concessions is extended to convicts under sentence. With this new regulation, and in 1882, under the leadership of Governor Pallu de la Barrière, wishing to humanize the prison, the pace of granting concessions increases sharply until exasperated free settlers obtain, from 1886, more rigor. This results in a fall in the number of the beneficiaries. There was also a policy of transportation of women - volunteers - because the colony had few women willing to marry released convicts.

The climax of the transportation is in 1885, when the prison administration represents nearly 700 agents who supervise 7600 convicts and 1900 released. Most convicts serve their sentences in the penitentiary of Nou Island. The Penal Administration is very powerful. Independent in 1875, it became a sort of state within a state. It manages many prisons: Nou island, Ducos, Noumea, Isle of Pines, Ouegoa, Canala, etc. As it needs a great quantity of land this administration has been assigned a land bank which reached 110,000 hectares. This is only partially used, but it contributes to serious spoliation against Kanaks, major cause of the insurrection of 1878..

Deportation is a political sentence that helps move away opponents or rebels to the government. Between 1872 and 1880, 4,300 deportees arrive in New Caledonia, following convictions against insurgents of the Paris Commune in 1871. These deportees are confined primarily to the Isle of Pines until 1880, when a general amnesty law allowed them to leave. Less than 40 families decide to settle in Noumea.

After the uprising of Sheikh El Mokrani in Algeria, about a hundred Kabyles are also deported in 1871 to the Isle of Pines. They are amnestied in 1895, but many of them remain and founds Caledonian families. Maghreb deportees are nearly 3000 and the « Caledoun » exhibition which was dedicated to them in 2011, at the Arab World Institute in Paris, shows how a womanless community becomes integrated, in one or two generations, into the demographic landscape. Statistically, their descendants are all Europeans or mixed-race, born in the archipelago, and better known by the derogatory term "Caldoches".

Some Kanak leaders are deported to Nou Island, like the chief of Boulouis tribe in 1868. Others are sent to Tahiti, or even in Obock or Pulo Condor. At the same time, Tahitian or Wallisian leaders are deported to New Caledonia.

In 1885, a new law requires that, now, second offenders will be "relegated" in overseas territories. In total there will be over 4,000 men and 457 women relegated. Relegation places are the Isle of Pines (in the former municipalities of deportation) and Prony (for logging).

Caledonian prison was not populated by "Jean Valjean" of the other side of the world. Old Europe got rid of the dregs of society and the majority of convicts were probably disreputable people. Life was tough and probably demeaning in overcrowded dormitories. Those who escaped this condition and married, more lucky, hardworking or more intelligent than others, are the source of most of the peopling of the New Caledonian bush. We owe them the complexity of the bushman, which combines hardness and apparent submission to authority, mistrust towards the powerful and confidence in his relatives. These characteristics disappear over the generations, they have forged a particular character which also owes much to the Kanak attendance.

Escapes are numerous and most of the escapees are caught by the native police, some manage to reach Australia or to settle permanently in a tribe. Deaths from disease, mistreatment and accidents are common in the prison world.

The death register of the general hospital of Nou Island prison, dubbed the Paradou (today Hospital Albert-Bouquet) is unfortunately very informative. There are many cases of deaths that could have been avoided: because of caused diseases which led to death the "lazy" condemned, or the desperate ones who had tried to escape, suicides or alleged suicides, violent deaths between "comrades", deaths due to abuse of the native police or even deaths attributable to the arbitrary power of the supervisors. It is true that 1239 convicts and some released are buried in the cemetery of the main camp (1867-1876). Then 1,960 convicts are buried between 1876 and 1889 in the cemetery of the Marais. These 3,199 graves have disappeared today.

Most of the sick and injured prisoners never arrived at Paradou. Many died in prison farms or in mobile camps. To simplify their administrative tasks, many supervisors never mentioned the convicts killed during an escape, merely noting that they were dead because of "fevers."

History has preserved the memory of 139 executions during the colonial period, the vast majority involving convicts or ticket of leave men. The executioner Mace performs 54 executions, continuing his sinister profession after being himself released and rehabilitated. Some contracted labour are guillotined after the murders of compatriots or employers. The first execution takes place in1867. It concerns four New Hebrideans who had killed the Pascal family in Dumbea.

In 1894, Governor Feillet on orders from Paris, prepares public opinion to stop the convoys of convicts. Indeed, the colony lived largely from prison: public works, redistributions of wages, supply of meat and other products (beans, corn), "Contracts of human flesh" with mining contractors. Free workers and missionaries are most favourable to the closure of the prison. The last convoy arrives in 1897. The last prisons were closed in 1922 and in 1931 New Caledonia is no longer a land of prison.

Those seventy years have involved the development of penal colonization. The most deserving are destined to concessions located on detention centres, the main ones being Bourail, La Foa, Farino, the Diahot, Pouembout and Prony. Concessions can be urban or rural; the rural are the most numerous. Finally, nearly 2000 released prisoners are sent on criminal concessions of three to five acres, with the materials needed to build a home-hut with one room and free food for eighteen months. Half of them are successful in their conversion into farming practicing a frugal mixed farming based on food crops of corn and beans.

Some historians consider that the rehabilitation by agricultural work was a failure, the "settlers by force" representing less than 5% of the convicts. We believe that this vast rehabilitation program was a success as 50% of beneficiaries are permanently implanted in the prisons centres of La Grande Terre.

Furthermore, transportation is the source of a large infrastructure (buildings, roads, bridges), as well as the arrival of many technicians, among the convicts or prison staff. Their knowledge and work greatly contributed to the development of the country. The Prison Service is, throughout the nineteenth century, a stable market of prime importance that ensures a certain standard of living for small settlers and ranchers. Thus, each year, Administration enters into a meat supply, thereby enhancing the Caledonian herds. When this market gradually disappears from 1897, the Administration supports the establishment of several canning factories, both in Ouaco and Noumea. Similarly, throughout the nineteenth century the Administration will finance the maintenance of secondary roads due to their usefullness in the crisscrossing of la Grande Terre. This measure, until the 1910s, has permitted the survival of many small farms, "settlers" surviving in their agricultural setbacks with jobs on road works.

Conversely, the mere presence of the released convicts distorts the relations between the French colonial administration and the Kanak countries. First, the Department of Colonies using the released in order to populate New Caledonia, creates deep antagonisms between "settlers against their will" and Kanaks horticulturists. Second, the Prison Administration creates an indigenous police force whose sole purpose is to return the escaped convicts. All former transported have experienced fear and hatred for those warriors who tracked and captured their brothers in misfortune in the deep valleys of the central mountain range. Third, the released are usually obliged to stay on La Grande Terre for the rest of their lives. They were extremely rough towards themselves, towards others, especially towards the Kanak. Indeed, they all remembered the reputation of the indigenous police, whose men did not hesitate to beat up recalcitrant prisoners, while released convicts unconsciously considered the Melanesian group as socially inferior.

The released are victims of history, as were, against their will, the New Hebrideans and Asians engaged or the free settlers deceived by false advertising. All suffer from the extremely coercitive pattern of the social hierarchy of the colonial period and transfer their bitterness on the Kanak world, which becomes doubly marginalized.

* Overshadowing the first people (1878 - 1918)

Many Kanak are unhappy because colonization takes their land, profanes their sacred areas and, more and more, treats them like inferior beings, the image of the "noble savage" leaving more and more room for the image of the "savage". Incidents take place regularly. Thus in 1877, because of drought, cattle destroyed the indigenous cultures on lands adjacent to the prison and sometimes in tribes.

It is therefore understandable that General Trentinian, in his explanatory report of the 1878 revolt, could write: *"If the Kanak hates the White, he hates even more their cattle."* In addition, in December begins the delimitation of the tribes in the region of La Foa. That is when the released Chêne, his Melanesian wife and their son are murdered on June 19, 1878, resulting in the arrest of the leaders of the region. On 25 and 26 June, Atai and his warriors attack La Foa, and Bouloupari and release the leaders. They also slaughter a hundred Europeans and destroy everything in their path.

On 27 June, Lieutenant Servan rallies warlord Nondo, from Canala, who thus finds the opportunity to fight against hereditary enemies. From now on Kanak choose their side, according to their traditional alliances. A majority of tribes joined the French. Fighting continue and extend, despite the death of Ataï on September 1st. Further outbreaks of revolt are reported on the west coast, because some tribes rose up out of fear of reprisals. In February 1879, Governor Olry promises to pardon insurgents who will surrender. On 3 June, the state of siege is raised between Bouloupari and Bourail. The toll was heavy. More than 1,000 dead: 200 Europeans and between 800 and 1000 Kanak. More than 1,500 of them are deported, some to Tahiti. Many settlers are ruined and authorities are questioning a moment about the future of the colony.

The failure of the revolt and the new demographic collapse of the Kanak people accentuate the overshadowing of the first people. Many young men died. Women are taken on the east coast. Many plantations are destroyed. Some try to forget their distress into alcoholism. The indigenous regime established in 1887, more restrictive in a settlement colony than in most colonies of exploitation, sets up an arsenal of coercitive measures to encourage Melanesians to stay in the reservations. History forgets a time the Kanak world to take account of the entry of New Caledonia on the world stage. Trade is the essential activity in New Caledonia. It is monopolized by the capital of the archipelago that becomes a trading post from the very beginning. Ships carrying goods to France or abroad and those that serve the entire archipelago are crossing in the harbour. The town has 7,000 inhabitants at the end of the nineteenth century, 14% of the total population. There are 137 licensed traders in 1903 the port has been modernized and new dock were opened in 1879.

In Noumea, trade businesses deal with French or foreign companies, then distribute the products in New Caledonia. One of these businesses takes soon a special place: the "Etablissements Ballande" that open their first store on rue de l'Alma in 1883, and retailing is practised in the interior. Trade businesses also support development by providing credit facilities to the settlers.

Army is everywhere to protect Noumea and the centres of colonization from depredations by escaped convicts, from pilfering by ticket of leave men and possible conflicts with Kanak. Life, both in Noumea and in the bush, is not always easy: this period is violent. Moreover, hurricanes and floods often challenge the fragile ease of settlers. Their health is generally good, despite leprosy that develops slowly in 1865, dengue fever appears in the 1880s and plague in 1900-1901.

At the same time, the settlers take time to live. The main spare time activities are: Sunday picnics, various card and board games, dancing, horse races and civilian or military ceremonies. Many activities are both fun and useful. Thus men like to hunt and fish. Taverns, numerous when considering the importance of alcoholism at the time, are places where information and rumours flow. Women do needlework while taking tea. Time passes differently in Noumea and in the bush, in the centres of colonization and stations, in mining camps of enlisted and in Kanak tribes.

* New Caledonia, mining land

In 1863, Australian prospectors find gold in Pouébo. The only interesting vein will be operated for nearly seven years at Fern Hill mine. In 1872, copper is discovered in Ouégoa areas. In 1880, the Lucky Hit chromium mine is worked near Plum. Later chromium is found in the mountains of the Tiébaghi range.

From 1896 to 1912, New Caledonia is the third largest producer of chromium. As soon as 1883 mining permits of concessions for extraction of cobalt are increasing. Such concessions are operated in Moneo, Koumac, Mont-Dore and Canala. But production, without competition until 1905, collapses in 1910. Many other minerals have been mined: iron in Prony, manganese near Voh.

The mining engineer Jules Garnier arrives in Noumea in 1863 to conduct a geological expedition for the imperial government. He notes in September 1864 in Dumbéa: *"The rock is also accompanied by a green material that is bonded to its surface, nickel? »*. This ore is soon called garnierite. It will be mined in 1873 in Mont-Dore by settler Coste. The first work is done with pickaxes in underground tunnels, and later in quarries.

The mining history of the colony will be punctuated by periods of hope and passion, almost irrational, then by sudden depressions resulting in economic crises, all the more visible as the archipelago is sparsely populated. Due to the lack of local important capital, all major projects are built on French financing or English, or Australian. Many companies were involved in nickel mining. Only two of them still exist today, Société Le Nickel and Ballande.

Nickel has been the great Caledonian speculation, when prospectors could register concessions they then sold to companies founded to exploit «King Nick". *Newspaper "Le Moniteur de la Nouvelle Calédonie" evokes it in 1875: "Do you believe in nickel? There is a safe bet that, if this question had been addressed to you only one year ago, you would have mischievously looked at your interlocutor, asking yourself whether he was serious or not. If you do not believe it, go and visit Mr Hankar's mine, in Canala.*

And Eugene Bridle added: *"Everyone began to dream of breath-taking emerald-coloured waterfalls; everyone wanted to have his mine or his share of a mine ... One could only see in the streets, but mainly in bars which are always full, people pulling out of pocket a sample of the precious ore. The more it is green, the more it is rich.*

In 1877, Jules Garnier raises capital, goes into partnership with an industrial from Septèmes-tles-Vallons (Bouches-du-Rhône) and opens the first New Caledonian smelter on Chaleix promontary. This plant provides mattes with a 60-70% nickel content and this new market encourages "small miners" to increase production. Nickel fever is approaching its climax as world prices have soared because of the increasing use of this mineral, primarily for surgical instruments and watches and finally armouring. It is now clear that the most important deposits are in Thio, Houaïlou and Népoui.

The massive exportation of Caledonian ore on large sailing ships, the Cape Horners, is the origin of the first "overproduction" crisis. The whole colony is feeling the effects of this crisis: farmers are without funds, shopkeepers have insolvent debtors, and the local budget has difficulties in collecting of taxes.

The consumption collapses and the first New Caledonian bank, the Banque de Nouvelle Calédonie, went bankrupt in November 1877. For the first time, the State supports the nickel economy, also suspends the 25 Franc tax related to the annual mining permits, and the tax on exportation of cobalt and nickel.

And one wonders if the Kanak revolt of 1878 does not find one of its many origins in the return of some settlers to their rural concessions, as the lack of financial resources do not facilitate the maintenance of fences.

Jules Garnier, engineer who proposes a smelting process similar to that of smelting iron (French Company for the treatment of ores of nickel, copper, cobalt and others) and John Higginson, great tycoon in New Caledonia (Society Higginson, Hanckar and Co.) merge their companies in order to create the Society Le Nickel on 10 May 1880. Soon, Higginson, being in difficulty, sells his shares to the Rothschild family, who controls SLN until the economic crisis of 1973-1975. John Higginson, who was the first to have a "human flesh contract" from the Penal Administration, sells his forced labourers to the SLN.

Thirty years later, the Société des Hauts Fourneaux de Noumea (owned by Ballande) creates in 1910, on the Doniambo headland, site of the current SLN, the only smelter still existing a hundred years later.

Mining lands being very poor agricultural land, their exploitation causes little land expropriation. The Kanak, usually poorly paid, generally accept to work on mines, just the time to acquire the goods required for a Great Custom. This is why, manufacturers use convicts through "human flesh contracts" made with the Penal Administration and the Chan Dang (shackled), that is to say Asian indentured labour. And an anonymous journalist of La France Australe declares on November 8, 1890: *"The regulation of labour cannot be the same in the colonies than in France, because there is a question of race. We can not apply the same principles to races that differ not only by origin but by their intellectual level. Impose the condition of the commitment to a European, would violate the individual liberty that he considers as its most sacred right."*

* The second wave of free colonization (1894-1903)
The capital has grown strongly throughout the second half of the nineteenth century due to the Penal Administration that represented jobs, investments and constructions. Also, infrastructure of Noumea is superior to those of other colonial cities of comparable size. The shops are numerous. Import-export stores like Ballande, Barrau, Béchade or Société Havraise Caledonienne are prosperous. Leisure are numerous: the bandstand, Chenevier and Hickson cinemas, horse races, picnics on nearby beaches, regattas, etc.
At the end of the nineteenth century, free settlers are very few. In addition, disorders caused by the insurrection of 1878 caused the departure of some of the farmers settled in the bush. Some released remain in place to whom Administration had allocated a plot of land. Paul Feillet, arrived in 1894, is surprised by the weakness of the free population. He said before the General Council: *"We are and we must be a colony of settlement."*
Sent by the Ministry to *"close the tap of dirty water"*, this enterprising Governor knows that he must propose alternatives

to the economic downturn related to the gradual departure of the largest employer in New Caledonia, the Penal Administration. Initially he takes steps to populate this territory by recruiting in France. Then, he launches major works like the extension of the wharf in Noumea or the project of a Noumea-Bourail railway that finally doesn't go beyond Paita.

The French administration launches a call for volunteers, farmers preferably, having a minimum capital of 5,000 gold francs permitting a family to live until the first harvest. The currency of the colony is the French Franc. After the failure of the "Marchand Bank" the "Banque de l'Indochine" opens in 1888 a branch that is granted the monopoly of issuing bank notes. They are denominated in French francs on Indochina banknotes overloaded "Noumea." Soon, three hundred families answer the call and disembark, after two months at sea, on the docks of Noumea.

Upon arrival, the Administration gives them concessions between 10 and 25 hectares, on part of which Governor Feillet recommends the cultivation of coffee, which is the "nickel of agriculture." But difficulties caused by isolation, poor soils, sometimes by inexperience of some settlers in agricultural work, and especially the collapse of coffee prices in 1900, lead to the relative failure of the "Plan Feillet".

Its effects are further reduced by the introduction of a disease of coffee in the late 1900s, *Hemileia vastatrix*. As noted by Faustine Bernut: *"During several successive years to 1908-1910, there was the terrible hémilia, coffee diseases, which ruined many families in the bush and did not spare my father since he nearly lost his fortune. It was terrible. New Caledonia was totally affected, especially growing areas coffee: In the beginning people replanted, but the coffee was dying inexorably. People had a vegetable garden, chicken, a pig, but they relied on coffee to provide them a living: it was money that was returning regularly every year on fixed dates. "*

Transportation between the properties and villages are still by mule trails or waggon trails and communications are always performed by sailing around the island. This subsidized ship, drops anchor every two weeks at the mouths of rivers, to serve outposts scattered all along New Caledonian coasts.

Under the "proconsul" Feillet, and along with the development of land colonization, the definitive establishment of the reservation system is decided, the "big cantonment" which delimits drastically all tribes. To do so, the Administration decides to impose a quota of three hectares per Kanak, knowing that the Melanesian population has halved since the imposition of indigenous reservations. Then it favours the regrouping of reservations. This causes undue displacements that still have an impact today, many clans do not have real land right where they live. The only positive aspect, Governor Feillet confirms in 1899 that the Loyalty Islands are totally indigenous reservations.

Governor Feillet critizises the mission and his friends Ballande for opposing his policy of Cantonment of Kanak. He pushes the notables of the only Masonic Lodge in Noumea, "l'Union Calédonienne", to come together in his politics. The Assembly, mostly conservative, temporarily switches to the Republican side and supports the Governor and his policy of free colonization.

Vexations are many and Kanak are at the bottom of the social current hierarchy, due to the triumphant Darwinism and racial prejudices of the time.

"Normalien " Marc Le Goupils, settler at the end of the nineteenth century in New Caledonia, wrote in 1928: *"Kanak will disappear without understanding in what capacity the white race had settled among them, or on what terms they wanted to live with them"*. Missionaries, both Catholic and Protestant, are then virtually alone in defending the Kanak against excesses increasingly present in the colonial period.

Chapter IV.
"Sleeping Beauty" (1918-1945)

The policy of public works undertaken by Feillet facilitates access of Noumea docks to ships and allows the opening of a railway line to Paita. These facilities give work to many released but unemployed convicts. But they greatly indebted the colony that dozes gradually.

On one hand, the programmed and gradual disappearance of the prison and the Penal Administration leads to a much lower number of civil servants and to a significant decline in orders from the State. Moreover, the 1918 victory turns out to be a deceptive victory. France is bloodless and a whole generation has been sacrificed, including New Caledonians. The French market collapses and the 1929 crisis brings the global, national and local economy into a long period of crisis.

* The Pacific Battalion and the First World War

The first contingent of Caledonian volunteers travel aboard the Sontay in April 1915. Volunteers of the Battalion of Native conscripts of the second contingent depart in June 1916. They are integrated into the Mixed Pacific Battalion, joigning Caledonians and Tahitians. In all, four contingents leave for France from 1915 to 1917.

From 1916 to 1918, the Pacific troups take part in many battles: in Barleux near Soissons, in « le Chemin des Dames », in Champagne, in the Second Battle of La Marne, in Vesle-et-Caumont, at Verdun. 2113 men had gone to join the 177 Caledonians mobilized on site in France, that is to say 1006 soldiers of European origin and 1,107 soldiers of Kanak origin. 456 Caledonians fall in action.

The conflict improve the nickel economy while reducing supply to the colony of manufactured goods. This is the time of "système "D" (ressourcefulness). The war, as in all the French colonial empire, allows the expression, often violent, of discontented colonized populations. In New Caledonia, misunderstanding between communities causes the "Kanak war" of 1917. Kanak are aware of being more and more away from their customs. The Status of Natives and confinement made them bitter and distrustful. Also, since 1896, occasional problems happen in the region of Koné. In 1914, the Chiefs of Mueo, Témala, Hienghène, Tiwaka are brought together by the Sorcerer Patéouand and chief Poindet Apengou for a great war pilou. Finally, the refusal of some Melanesians to go to military downsizing, encourage these leaders to schedule the hostilities, during a meeting at Tiendanite at the end of 1916. On February 17, 1917, pro-French tribes of Koniambo are attacked by Noël, the lesser chief of Tiamou. From that moment, insecurity reigns. Attacks of "stations" multiply in Pouembout, deep in the valley of Amoa, in the valley of the Tipindjé. The Kanak still use traditional weapons, and also guns legally purchased or stolen in the first lootings.

According to anthropologist Jean Guiart then intervenes the last event of ritual and war cannibalism: *"Contrary to what is being said ... eating of heart of man killed by Kaféat for deserting the cause of the insurgents, has been committed in Pukepaï, in chief Ty's home, the last supporter of the movement, and of whom he was the brother."*

The revolt remains confined to large rectangle Hienghène Poindimié Mueo, Voh. The last action of Noël, on September 9, is the attack of the military post of Voh. Helped by Caledonian and Tahitian soldiers on leave "the pacification expedition" continues until the death of Noël, killed by an Arab acquaintance in January 1918.

Historian Sylvette Boyer notes: *"The number of denunciations occurring since the beginning of the events, especially denunciations between Kanak ".* And in fact, this revolt against the excesses of land colonization is also a clanic war, a religious war, a war of witch doctors and a war of chiefs in which alliances and loyalties change according to local antagonisms.

In the nineteenth century, local revolts had first hit the region around Noumea. In 1878, spoliations by the pioneer front had led the warriors from the centre of la Grande Terre to rebel. In 1917, it was the last demarcations of reservations and the refusal to go and be killed on the opposite side of the world that lead the Kanak of northern New Caledonia to revolt.

Ten Europeans are murdered and approximately sixty insurgents. Incidentally, it appears that the obvious exaggeration of the events reports allows New Caledonian soldiers on leave and young conscripts not to board the boat to the trenches and the horrors of the Great War.

* A dual society

After World War I, New Caledonia is facing a serious economic crisis due to lower sales of nickel, which the Governor Guyon, who arrived in 1925, tries to remedy. A General Council was created in 1885, but its powers are limited, the Administration considering that local interests are not always compatible with the national interest. Especially, officials hardly admit that released and rehabilitated convicts or their children who grew up in the colony, can eventually become mayors and give orders to the police.

The City Council of Noumea now operates normally, political debates and conflicts with the government being carried forward to the General Council. The City Council can give priority to the strengthening and development of networks that make Noumeans' life easier: running water and wastewater, streets and sidewalks, gas streetlights and, later, electric.

However, the population of Noumea, which is 12 874 in 1906, is no more than 8994 in 1936. City revenues stagnate since that extra-ordinary revenues made possible by the gradual sale of town lots, were exhausted due to lack of available land. To perpetuate the resources coming from land, the Council has developed a policy of renting the last municipal lands.

In 1926, textile workers in northern France that are called "Nordistes" (219 people) settled, especially in the Moindou and Gouaro (Bourail) areas in order to grow cotton. This is the latest attempt to agricultural colonization of New Caledonia. Due to lack of resources and organization, this experiment fails. The country is no exception, in fact, to the global crisis. Some Caledonians fall into great misery. Coffee does sell anymore, the centre of Yate is closed.

In 1937, the first steps of the Popular Front (40 hours work week and paid annual holidays) are applied to The territory. The year 1939 seems to open new horizons to New Caledonia: a seat in parliament is about to be granted.

Life is hard for the settlers. Crops of corn and beans cannot be sold to the Penal Administration and coffee prices have collapsed. Land owners develop mixed farming and live more and more self-sufficiently. They find additional resources through the mills, maintenance of roads for the Administration or the sale of deer skins.

An inventory after a death, in Tendea (Farino) in 1941, gives us an idea glimpse of farm equipment and property owned by most of the modest settlers *"A cast iron pot, five cast iron casserole dishes, a pot-tailed, a frying pan, a cast iron kettle, two enamelled pans, a enamelled jug, a wooden mixer, six ducklings, an axe, a ripsaw, a roll of metal cloth, two crowbars, a shovel, a screen for coffee, a dobby wire mesh, a crankshaft, six litres of honey, two hoes, a hand saw, a log saw, a winnowing machine, four sheets of corrugated iron. A 3 room house with veranda all around covered in sheet metal, walls covered with stuces. A wooden kitchen covered in sheet metal. A hen run covered in corrugated iron, a corn crusher, seven chicken, a rooster, about ten hectares of land."*

New Caledonians supplement their diet by hunting and fishing. Interest in beaches and swimming in the sea remains moderate because so few people can swim and sharks are feared. Tropical sun also is feared and wearing a hat is widespread.

The 1929 crisis causes the collapse of the de Béchade Company and forces Ballande Company to sell their foundry in Doniambo to the SLN. Credit is scarce and the bankruptcy of many small settlers forced their families to settle in the mining centres or in the capital. Economic and social stagnation prevails in the archipelago.

Communications are difficult because of the terrain of the island and families are isolated. The "Tour de côte" (coastal shipping) is the means of transporting goods throughout the first half of the twentieth century. Locally, heavy goods are transported by teams of oxcarts.

The "Messageries Automobiles", founded in 1904, ensure daily connections between Noumea and Moindou with a "motor car". The Moindou- Bourail section is by car hypo mobile (sulky). The road is paved only a third of the way, the bus or "patache" leaves at 5am from Noumea, arriving at night in Moindou (136 km).

Its manager, F. Garcia, the founder of the Caledonian automobile noted in 1934: "I developed in the communities served by our buses produce trade, vegetables, poultry, eggs and seafood ... It is from this point that vegetable gardening started to develop. This success allowed small traders to buy our vans and continue for themselves the traffic we had operated ... The car has been the source of a greater good. "

Official history mentions less and less the first people. It has not disappeared as predicted by some observers. The Kanak countries live, since the Kanak 1917 war, folded in on themselves, enclosed in the regulations of the indigenous regime, regularly extended and completed every ten years since 1887. To move out of a reservation requires a prior administrative authorization, chores are instituted or "natives" are subject, in 1900, to the poll tax.

This very restrictive straitjacket is acceptable because the Melanesian population drops to the level of 1921 and represents only 27,000 people, including 17,000 over the entire Grande Terre. Throughout the colonial period, Ouvea (2000), Mare (3000) and Lifou (5000) maintained their populations, because the French government prefered to concentrate land settlement on la Grande Terre.

The Kanak population collapse is explained primarily by microbial shock, which appears from the mutual discovery and continues to the end of the nineteenth century. Revolts, with the notable exception of 1878 lead to little direct mortality, but they are followed by many deaths related to the destruction of huts and cultures, as well as injuries from repressions and "evictions". Finally, the settling of Kanak on reservations, about thirteen percent of the Mainland, results in lasting despair that is visible through the rapid development of alcoholism. The one of the reasons behind the dilapidated state of Melanesian society. It was not until the 1920s to see a slow but steady population recovery. Thus, after the Second World War, the New Caledonian population consists of over a third of Kanak, a third of Europeans and an "elastic" third of Asians. The progressive departure of Indonesians and Vietnamese in the late 1950s will change the demographic order.

* One third of the population is Asian

Meanwhile, the need for labour explains the arrival of Asians in the late nineteenth century. A first convoy of Japanese under contract arrives for SLN on 18 January 1892. At the end of their contract, many of them want to settle in order to do, as they are legally authorized, trading, fishing, agriculture or gardening. In addition, two colonies respond favourably to the immigration policy under contract: French Indochina and Dutch West Indies. The first Indochinese arrive in 1891 and the first Javanese arrive Feb. 16, 1896.

The Japanese, as protected foreigners, are subject to a preferential treatment because they come with individual contracts. Since 1900, the Japanese access - at the end of their four-year contract - the freedom of establishment and free movement.

Between 1892 and 1919, more than 6,800 Japanese arrive in New Caledonia as indentured labour. Conditions remain tough, ten hours of work per day with an hour break for lunch and the obligation to accept two additional hours paid, if necessary.

The individual contract type, much shorter than the indentured contract, includes sections very different for items that are not always to the benefit of the contracting party: *"Article III. Wages will be paid directly to the worker and monthly; Article V. The worker will have to defray all his other needs (food, clothing, etc.); Article XIII. The worker will pay himself the travel from and to Japan. "*

This community is the only one to quickly count a large number of free workers and their success, in agriculture, commerce or industry, partly explains the rigor with which they are arrested and deported to Australia at the beginning of World War II, their property being sequestered.

While most of Asian indentured labour are struggling on mines, some are hired on breeding stations by public services (construction, road repair, etc.), on ships or in private, especially for women. Indeed, it was planned that each convoy would include approximately 10% of women in order to avoid problems of manners and to facilitate eventual installation. Thus, the loose black trousers and the brown blouses of Indochinese women become an integral part of the landscape, like the conical Annamese hat.

Despite often very harsh conditions of life and work, these workers continue to arrive at Freycinet island and go to " the Orphanage depot" to find an employer, because the average salary is 12 piastres for men and 9 piastres for women was, if one believes governor Guyon, thirty times higher than they could get in Indochina. Part of the salary is withheld by employers to form the "savings" they receive only at the time of departure.

Their contract includes for example the precise list of clothing to be allocated to them every year or the amount of food that is delivered to them daily. These articles provide normal conditions of life to the indentured labour, but the reality is often quite different. Food actually consists generally of rice and a few pieces of meat, often   accomodation is unhealthy and the regulatory blanket is so thin and of such poor quality that the entire colony names it "ration blanket."

As usual in terms of indentured labour, they are accompanied by criminal penalties. Absenteeism, work refusal and insubordination are reasons to punish the workers to 8 to 60 days of discipline workshops in the capital. As a judgment and a long trip were necessary, most employers, not always sure of their right, preferred to use their own forms of discipline, fines or corporal punishment. But why did they accept this life of misery?

Jean Vanmai believes that *"the wages, ridiculous nowadays, but so high for them in that time, by saving well and they knew how to, allowed them to buy a piece of land and build a small house when they would return back home. They were young, life would start over again. "*

The quotas were organized by the Administration in order to monitor the evolution of the New Caledonian economy and therefore the labour market. Furthermore, caution led civil authorities to diversify labour sources to avoid the formation of excessive ethnic minorities. This same concern for balance explains the difficulty of the procedures that the Indochinese had to undertake if they wanted to settle. In fact, only 139 of them managed to get strong envied status of free resident before 1939.

Indochinese indentured workers arrive massively, especially after World War I, as the Japanese are less sought often and that the situation has become so bad in Indochina that commitment becomes a real alternative to unemployment. Important quotas, from 500 to 900 workers, arrive and soon steamships on the Saigon-Noumea line carry the human goods in both directions.

The first contingent of 170 Javanese arrive in Noumea by the steamer St. Louis, chartered by the firm Ballande, after twenty days at sea, in 1896. Each of them have a registration ID number that long will be their marital status. Their daily diet is composed of: 1 kilo of rice, 250 g salted fish or 300 g of meat, 24 g salt, 50 g of sugar and 3 grams of tea. Until 1903, the Javanese work on coffee plantations, among farmers and as domestic help.

The problem of labour on mines is far from being solved, while the coffee culture was experiencing a severe crisis, they are then hired for the haulage and transport of ore. At the end of their contract (five years and subsequently renewable for three-year)s, they return to their original colony. As for those who wish to stay, they not only loose their right to repatriation, but they must pay the costs of introducing a new worker. Few are those who obtain free residence established under conditions, in 1909, for the Asian.

Each community is bound by slightly different contracts. For example, that of 1920 applied to Javanese has an article n ° 5 as follows: *"leave will be 1 day per week and 3 days on the occasion of the Javanese New Year"*. Considered to be workers and docile, they are often treated better than others involved and the General Council is favourable for them to achieve free residence. It is true that New Caledonian leaders did not wish that «*this workforce left with their savings at the expiration of their contract*» while François Doumenge noted that the Dutch Governor wanted a restriction on repatriation of savings, fearing that *"some elements of homecoming raise claims movements and reactions after receiving higher incomes and better living and working conditions."*

The real settlement of Javanese and Tonkinese dates to World War II. The break in contacts between Gaullist New Caledonia and Indochina, prevents then any repatriation for five years, despite many regrets or even strikes. In 1945, the time commitment of the thousands of men and women is greatly lapsed. The French Government is providing on 15 June of the same year the free residence to all contract workers. Their children then acquire the French nationality and become part of the New Caledonian society.

* The beneficial impact of World War II (1940-1945)

Despite Petain's supporters, a pro-De Gaulle committee is founded by New Caledonians favourable to the ideas of Free France. General de Gaulle sent Henri Sautot, who has just obtained the rallying of the New Hebrides and officially announces the rallying of New Caledonia to Free France September 19, 1940.

Many volunteers join the Pacific Expeditionary Corps. New Caledonians, Tahitians and New Hebrideans form the Pacific Battalion. They combat in the sands of the desert (Bir-Hakeim) and in Italy (Monte Casino), and they joinin the liberation of France. Other commandos also fighting in and participated in the D day landing of June 6, 1944 in Normandy. Many Caledonians also serve in the Free French Naval Forces.

Many Kanak leaders push their "subjects" to enlist to defend France, to show their goodwill and give an opportunity for young adults to prove they are warriors like their ancestors. The administration multiplies the promises so that young Kanak incorporate in number the Pacific batallion.

The High Chief of the North of the island of Mare, Henri Naisseline, is the first Kanak traditional Chief to provide his support to Charles de Gaulle in the fight against the Axis powers. He hoisted the French flag marked with the Cross of Lorraine in the tribe of Nétché on October 11, 1940 and opened lists for commitment of volunteers for his subjects aged 18 to 45. At the same time, he launched a radio appeel to the other chiefs on October 16, 1940: *"With light-coloured eyes and pride, the natives of free New Caledonia must rush to General de Gaulle to defend the honour of the tricolour flag that represents the spirit of freedom and justice. »* At the end of November, he arrived in Noumea with 80 volunteer Maré

Islanders he hopes for reward to rallying, namely obtaining for Kanak, after the conflict, full French citizenship and thus the total repeal of the native code, as he explains in a letter written to General de Gaulle on October 31: *"I have appealed to all the natives of New Caledonia. Our colour and our language are not French but our heart is. These natives all French by the heart remain deeply attached to the Motherland [...] I ask you to ensure that, in recognition of our gesture and sacrifice of the lives of those who, out there, will surely fall, that he is given the right to acquire the title of French citizen. "*

To counter the Japanese advance in the Pacific, the US Forces, supported by New Zealanders and preceded by an Australian commando, make New Caledonia the backbone of the defence and of the Allied counter-attack. On 12 March 1942, the "Poppy Force," a large convoy of 18,000 men, under the command of General Patch, arrives in Noumea, which then becomes the headquarters of the Pacific. Airfields are built (Tontouta, Plaine des Gaiacs ...). Ammunition and fuel depots occupy all available docks. Hospitals are located in Anse Vata, in La Conception, in Dumbéa, to the north of Bourail, on the east coast and in the far north. In fact, New Caledonia became the "rear aircraft carrier", motionless and unsinkable, of Allies in Melanesia.

The Third New Zealand Division, under the command of General H.E Barrowclough, arrives in New Caledonia on November 11, 1942. Soon the kiwi soldiers colloquially nicknamed the island "Necal", pronounced "nickel" in English. Almost 17 000 New Zealanders have the task of defending the northern half of the island starting beyond Moindou. This is possible thanks to the strong motorized division: 3377 vehicles including 2016 cars, jeeps and trucks and 507 tractors or universal carrier. The H.Q. is installed in Bourail in the "base wallahs."

Americans introduce mechanization to agriculture. They clear the land with bulldozers and plant with mechanical appliances.

Contacts were establishd with tribes who receive salaries in dollars, of an amount previously unknown.

The American HeadQuarters favours racial segregation and therefore treats New Caledonian, Asian and Kanak employees differently. Some officers even propose the opening of two brothels, one for European soldiers and one for black soldiers. The French gendarmerie, called upon to facilitate the implementation of this project and to find volunteer Kanak women, refused to associate with this record that remained in boxes. From 1944, the theater of operations moves away from New Caledonia. The year 1946 was marked by the departure of the last GI's and the return of the Free French Volunteers. New ways of life appear and New Caledonians discover whisky, jeeps, jazz or agricultural machinery. Also, the time of the Americans will long be seen as a time of plenty.

At the departure of Americans Noumea inherits *quonset huts*, metal half-moon, convenient and but hot to inhabit, as well as paved roads joining the various villages. New Caledonians, thanks to "dollars-touques" meaning dollars earned during the war and kept in metal cans, enter an economic cycle of prosperity. Meanwhile, barriers between social groups are collapsing. The descendants of convicts are no longer marginalized, more and more children of rural settlers will work in Noumea. As for Kanak, they have met some black soldiers who ordered Europeans, others worked on U.S. or New Zealand bases. All wished to see liberalize the regime of reservations, because of their slow demographic renewal.

Part three
Present-day,
From autonomy to decolonization inside France

Chapter V.
An original decolonization (1945-1988)

The contemporary political history of New Caledonia will be truly written only tomorrow. It should be noted that, due to the conflicting chronology of the colonial period and to the opprobrium cast on New Caledonia as a former penal colony, history was long hidden.

Indeed, it implied to mention two taboos: the land theft and the criminal backgrounds of the majority of the old French families living in the bush. Those two elements are used to explain both the Kanaks' mistrust of the European world and their long unknown alliance with the majority of small Caledonian settlers. It is true that the descendants of settlers despite themselves, as much as the Kanaks, had a defiance at law and its representatives. "The Caledonian Union" appeared, literally, as a political party and, figuratively, in spirits, against the image of the State and its allies, the big economic interests of import-export and metalworking industry.

* Towards greater autonomy (1945-1958)
Even before the establishment of the Fourth Republic, the Brazzaville conference shows the desires of the future provisional government of the French Republic to undertake reforms. Indeed, Free French colonial officials who organize it for General de Gaulle, are the initiators of the "new colonial policy," consider that the Empire must be modernized and inequalities arising from economic exploitation, reduced, by increasing the role Administration considered as liberating individuals. Meanwhile, they do not imagine any political

emancipation of the components of the Empire, just as they relied on it for the reconquest of France.

The reform policy has been applauded by Caledonian Gaullists elites who give priority to financial reforms. Thus, the President of the General Council of New Caledonia, Pierre Bergès says about the Brazzaville conference in his opening speech in 1945: *"it may be called the French imperial charter... in this framework ... we claim, with respect, the right to be the masters of expenditure financed by the local budget. "*

It is then in accordance with the social reformism born during the Liberation of France and under the pressure of a local communist political discourse able to influence a large part of the electorate - a third of French citizens vote for the PCF (French Communist Party) after Liberation – that Governors and the General Council examine the needed statutory and socio-economic evolutions. Besides, the first General Council elected after the war is the most leftist one of the New Caledonian history until this day.

From 1945 the status of the native population is deleted. All inhabitants of New Caledonia become French citizens. Melanesians gradually access to the right to vote. According to the constitution of the Fourth Republic, dated October 2, 1946, New Caledonia is no longer a colony but becomes an Overseas Territory (TOM), represented in Paris by a deputy, Roger Gervolino, and an advisor of the Republic elected in 1947, Henri Lafleur.

On a fiscal and financial level, war tax (1945) and then head tax (1947) are abolished. Regarding labour organization, conscriptions finally disappear on May 3, 1946 at the initiative of the central government .The *indentured labour contracts* are finally abolished in 1948. The Administration, because of the constant lack of labour, delays as much as possible the return of the Asians who had been recruited prior to the interruption of maritime communications with Asia in 1940. From 1954 and the fall of Dien Bien Phu, an «anti-Viet campaign" takes place. Finally, all those who wish are repatriated without charge between 1958 and 1963: 3786 Tonkinese return to Vietnam; 972 choose to stay and integrate locally. Indonesians predominantly choose to stay in New Caledonia. The end of cheap labour market obliges mine operators to mechanize their activity: then they import mechanical diggers, trucks, automated laboratories and conveyor belts. With the end of the war in Algeria, more than a thousand *Pieds Noirs* (Black Feet) settled - without assistance - in New Caledonia.

In the electoral field, the French government authorizes violations of the principle of absolute equality by introducing some "special laws" in the legal domain. Indeed, on the one hand the former subjects of the Empire are more numerous in the French Union than French citizens living in France (distribution of seats in Parliament). On the other hand, in New Caledonia, all told, indigenous and some formely indentured labour Asians, who had acquired French nationality, are as numerous as the settlers (allocation of seats to the General Council).

New Caledonians of European descent, only voters yesterday, are worried. Melanesian notables do not want to reappraise the colonial period, but they want access to full citizenship and to participate to public life, in order that reserves remain inalienable and that their material way of life improves. Following the gradual departure of Asians recruited between 1936 and 1940 and the disappearance of this type of community contract, the Kanak population obtains a small majority in the 1950s

Henri Bonneaud, Conservative chairman of the General Council from 1947 to 1951, remains very clear about the actual powers of the institution. *"We are also governed by custom Mr. Duplat, custom that wants we make decisions never enforced, and this lasts since sixty years now"*

The electoral status quo, favourable to European voters and negotiated by Representative Roger Gervolino lasts until

1951. Indeed the law of 23 May 1951 widening the native Electoral College in the territories under the Ministry of "France d'Outre-Mer", is made applicable to New Caledonia, to the surprise of local elected officials. This decision is made, not to satisfy the demands of the two local Kanak religious associations having political purposes, but to allow an unknown candidate, non Gaullist, Maurice Lenormand, to beat in an election the two Gaullists candidates considered de facto as enemies of the Fourth Republic. 60% of Melanesians of voting age access the voting right, that represents 45% of the New Caledonian electorate. Finally, the decree of 22 July 1957 establishes universal suffrage in New Caledonia

The second debate, concomitant of the first, is about equality or the weighting of votes. Most New Caledonians of European descent are favourable to double Electoral College that would underestimate the electoral weight of Melanesians. Finally, the implementing act of 25 October 1946, promulgated November 12, 1946 by the very young Fourth Republic does not include the dual college.

In the elections of 1953, a large gathering of "small against the big" is named Caledonian Union (UC). This multi-ethnic and multi-religious party led by Maurice Lenormand, elected representative since 1951, will dominate politics for 20 years. This party formalizes the alliance between modest whites (penniless settlers and unionized employees) and two associations representing the Kanak population: the Catholic UICALO (Union of Indigenous Caledonians Friends of Liberty in Order) and the Protestant AICLF (Association of Indigenous Loyaltians, Caledonians and French).

On February 8, 1953 elections give fourteen seats to the Caledonian Union (UC) out of the twenty-five that make up the General Council. UC had presented fourteen candidates, all are elected, including nine Melanesians. Maurice Lenormand then says: *"If the French Union fails in New Caledonia, with all the favourable conditions combined here, where will it be successful and become a living and compelling reality? "*

Meanwhile, Maurice Lenormand awkwardly decides not to involve the minority in the management of political affairs, as was his right. In debates about France and its offshoot that was the French Union, the Caledonian Union, throughout this period (1953-1958), has a "national" discourse while using a leftist phraseology. The motto of the party newspaper," L'Avenir Caledonian" is: *"The truth in the service of the people."*

Maurice Lenormand repeatedly marks his real attachment to France saying, for instance, in 1957 during the preparation of the framework-law: *«New Caledonia is French and will remain French by the perpetual and irrevocable wish of its inhabitants"*.

At the same time, the motto for the Caledonian Union: is: *«Two colours, but one people»*. This motto is a real revolution in attitudes since it calls into question the previous classifying schemes of the New Caledonian society that separated communities and strongly organized the society into a hierarchy.

In 1956, the Caledonian Union becomes an effective electoral machine in the service of an ambitious social upgrading and of development. Elected in 1951 with 36.7% of the vote, Maurice Lenormand, similar to MRP, was re-elected with 61% of New Caledonian votes. He is no longer, as say his opponents, «Kanaks' representative", but the representative for all Caledonian communities.

In 1956, the Socialist Gaston Defferre, who has become Minister of France d'Outre-mer, wants real reform, considering necessary to act quickly and effectively in order to maintain the confidence of representatives and of residents of overseas territories.

The "Defferre law", framework law, was passed in France on June 23, 1956. Intended for colonies in Africa, it will be applied the following year in New Caledonia. Five basic novelties: universal suffrage becomes really universal, Public Service is fleshed out and separated between the State and Territory; the Government Council replaces the Governor regarding the executive for local issues; the Ministers run their sectors; the Territorial Assembly has legislative power.

New Caledonia, a former colony of settlement soon rallied to Free France, enjoys a privileged status. Thus, fiscal and budgetary autonomy of New-Caledonia allows it to oppose the repeated attempts of the administration to establish the income tax, while the General Council considers the cost of living was too high; And in fact, the territorial budget, which has the merit of being balanced, was then much more important than the state budget in New Caledonia. So, Henry Bonnard liked to repeat this saying he had made his: *"The one who pays gives the orders."*

All this explains why Representative Lenormand, just as Polynesian autonomist representative Pouvanaa, refuses to vote for the "framework law", considering that the situation of Pacific territories may deteriorate if this law is applied uniformly.

On February 10, 1957, when the "Assemblée Nationale" votes on first reading the decrees relating to State services, representative Lenormand undertakes to frontally attack the decrees implementing the framework law. In these decrees thirty-three departments are declared state departments and, by overlapping, some other local departments are placed under guardianship. Especially for all these services, Caledonia will have to pay a levy of operation, which unduly restricts its budgetary and fiscal freedoms.

All New Caledonian political parties are in this analysis which has its justification in the fact that since 1900 France obliges the budget of New Caledonia to pay almost all operating expenses and investment.

The head of the local political opposition, Henri Bonneaud, in February 1957, sends the following telegram to Maurice Lenormand « I *confirm my full agreement with the protest of*

General Council against anything that could undermine freedoms already acquired by New-Caledonians. I agree on a councillors meeting to protest in this way"

Finally, the decrees concerning the State departments are not altered; the Ministry considers that, as they were common to all the territories, they could not be changed. However, the institutional decree is amended. The framework law does not call into question the interests of France, the chief of Staff of the Minister of France d'Outre-mer specifies to the Minister of Economic Affairs: *"All precautions are taken to safeguard the general interests of the Republic».* Indeed, there is no internal autonomy but an administrative autonomy.

After winning the local elections in October 1957, representative Lenormand becomes Vice-President of the Government Council. For the first time, local political majority has the means to carry out its policies. For the first time, the political debate between majority and opposition is no longer about electoral matters, but on the operation of this new administrative autonomy.

Meanwhile, the creation of a strong currency, the CFP franc, supported by France, and the opening of the Territory, with the licencing of shipping and airlines, allow a development of the economy. The changes due to World War II then persist, with the launch of many major projects such as dams in Yate and Dumbea, electrification of villages and road improvements. For these sites, many "rural whites" and Kanak begin to leave the bush and Polynesians from Wallis and Tahiti are recruited.

This comes as the Kanak population curve begins to recover. Guiart considers a WHO program for fifty years, bringing the entire New Caledonian population to be treated with long-acting penicillin would have eradicated yaws and also, at the same time, gonorrhoea in Kanak community. *"The women started at that time to have children and to repopulate the villages, which is the cause of independence in other regions and of political problems in New Caledonia, starting with the simple fact that the Melanesian population, so long steady at a low level, doubled every thirty years. »*

* The climax, then the decline of autonomy (1958-1974)

The 1958 troubles in Algeria and in France lead to early elections. The majority of the New Caledonian population confirms its confidence in the Caledonian Union. MP Maurice Lenormand, carried by a large majority, made the choice to engage in the struggle against the state, knowing that this attitude would earn him great popularity with the New Caledonian population. He can not foresee that the change of majority in France, in 1958, will lead to the rapid hardening of positions by the state.

The conservative opposition is concerned about the real desire or fantasy of the Caledonian Union to want more autonomy. Also, on June 18, 1958, an event is organized by the *Républicains Sociaux* (future UNR) with the help of many bushmen to reverse the local government or at least make it move back.

The High Commissioner receives a delegation that exposes him two claims: the rewriting of the institutions created by the framework law, in order to reduce the power of the local majority (collective responsibility of the Government Council, and his election by proportional representation); the removal of some metropolitan officials recruited by the Administration Council. Like in Algeria on May 13, 1958, the crowd elects a Vigilance Committee which is chaired by the Mayor of Noumea, Roger Laroque. This committee drafts the same day a "Message of territorial opposition to President of the Republic."

MP Lenormand goes into hiding until the republican order is restored by the State. As Caledonian Union criticizes the missed "coup" of June 18, General de Gaulle says: *"Well, but the question is not there. The question is why this event occurred. In other words, it is whether it is appropriate to provide solutions to the current situation and, if so, which*

ones? This is what my government is going to apply to doing
"And he would have added:" France can not give up New
Caledonia for strategic, economic, geographic, social and
human reasons. We still have a lot to do there. We'll do it
together. Gentlemen, thank you. "

The reformist and social policy of the Fourth Republic lived. The Fifth Republic will glorify the great France, giving to local populations, in the early years, the choice to stay in or to leave the French Community. Jacobinism prevails and independence of New Caledonia is gradually reduced to the strict minimum.

Thus in 1963 the Jacquinot law abolishes the ministries. The Government Council, reduced to five members, only has an advisory role to the Governor. In 1969, the Billotte laws are passed which reduces the powers of the Territory in the management of the mining area.

During this period, the standard of living of the Caledonians increases considerably with the development of State aids and the start of the mining boom in 1967. After the "era of transistors", the television era begins in 1965.

Melanesians of La Grande Terre, marked by the colonial period, continue to avoid working for Western companies. Islanders from the Loyalty Islands, who were not colonized strictly speaking, migrate more easily to Noumea. They have, through the mission schools, a relatively high level of education and they strongly desir to return home with money in the "suitcase" for their future marriage. The Lifuans work more generally in the Administration or in the Protestant church, People from Maré work as market gardeners and more generally as employees in the private, people from Ouvéa are seamen on vessels in the local fleet. It should be noted that Métis were the first to invest in the city or in the relations between the urban world and omnipresent rural world.

Since 1962, nickel prices are rising. the New Caledonian nickel ore production expands rapidly, reaching 7.5 million tons at the end of 1971. In Népoui the largest conveyor belt in the world (13 km) is assembled and in Poro an ore processing plant is built. Major works are undertaken to develop Noumea which receives the bulk of new immigrants.

In Noumea, capital inflows lead to an influx of populations: Europeans 5000, 3000 Tahitians, 2000 Wallis. This population boom, following the economic boom, has economic, social and political implications. Kanak are losing their demographic dominance and Caledonian Union loses power from 1972. Indeed this political party relies primarily on the Melanesian vote that becomes relatively less important, while many leaders - and thus tribes – join the local right because of the personality of Mr. Lenormand, of internal conflicts in Kanak countries and of prestige competitions.

Meanwhile, many small settlers and union members are facing the slow rise of Melanesian claims, concerning the expansion of reservations or their entering into the world of labour. At the same time, the local right wing has understood that the management of the city of Noumea and of the electoral majority in the first district are not sufficient to enable it to lead the destiny of the archipelago. It therefore integrates union members and Kanak leaders who appreciate General de Gaulle's prestige, by developing a social practice offset by the absence of income tax.

Meanwhile, New Caledonia continues to open up to the world. Thus the "fairy TV" arrives in to homes of greater Noumea in October 1965. The whole west coast is covered in 1969. The east coast receives the programs in 1972 and the Loyalty Islands in 1975. The programs length of Noumea-TV is initially two hours and a half. It reaches six hours in 1978. The use of satellite in 1975 revolutionizes the monitoring of national and international news. The first program broadcast from the studios comes in 1977 to mark the 11th cycling tour of New Caledonia. Colour TV arrives the same year and the first live program via satellite delights the World Cup football lovers in 1978.

The end of the Vietnam War and the fall of the dollar puts an end to the euphoria. Many Melanesians have not participated in prosperity and wonder about speculation and distribution of mining wealth. Meanwhile, the recession leads to the emergence of demands for independence. Indeed, the crisis of nickel leads to stagnation and unemployment, given that it primarily affects Kanak workers, less skilled than Europeans and considered less stable than Wallisians and Futunians. This direct competition for the least skilled jobs largely explains the latent antagonism between Melanesians and Polynesians.

In July 1969, a political association, the Red Scarves, challenges the authority of France. But the economic recession deepens in 1974 and causes bankruptcies and unemployment, accentuating the disagreements. In 1975, a pro-independence committee is created which includes youth groups, elected officials of the Multiracial Union and some elected Melanesians of the Caledonian Union, including MP Roch Pidjot.

* From the Kanak revival to demands for independence (1975-1984)

In 1975, the 2000 Melanesia festival, led by Jean-Marie Tjibaou, reaffirms the Kanak cultural identity. In an interview in April 1977 Tjibaou specifies the innovative work that is then undertaken: *"All the talks of the settlers, of the mission and of Administration, have induced in the traditional mentality a kind of shame; this is the feeling of alienation. One must be different to be a respectable man, an accepted man, a man of civilization, a man of technique, of strength, of gloss. In short, to become a man, you must deny your own culture."*

He adds: *"What is important is meeting itself, because it is unique, it has never happened in history, because there has never been the opportunity or the means to gather, through our custom, in such a short time, so many different people from different backgrounds. It needed this festival to allow the people from Bélep and those of the Isle of Pines to meet with the people of Ouvea»*

At the Bourail Congress, in 1977, the Caledonian Union takes position for independence in its statement of general policy on May 22, *"The VIII th Congress of Caledonian Union in Bourail on 21 and 22 of May 1977 decides, whatever it may cost, to make every effort to keep peace in the Territory, remaining true to the motto of the Movement, "two colours, one people"; It recognizes that Kanak are the first occupants of New Caledonia. Independence must ensure all their rights to Kanak. The autonomy, with a local executive with responsible ministers and an elected Government Council will involve all Caledonians in the management of the country. Autonomy should allow better confronting and solving Kanak problems in a process of decolonization. Autonomy, if faithfully accepted and respected by the French government, is the step that should normally lead the people of New Caledonia to independence. "*

The French government tries to appease the growing unrest by proposing a new status and a development plan, favouring Melanesian promotion and by launching a land reform. For his part, Jacques Lafleur brings together the vast majority of supporters of maintaining New Caledonia into the French Republic, in 1977, in the "Rassemblement Pour la Calédonie". This young party becomes the "Rassemblement Pour la Calédonie dans la République" (RPCR) in 1978. It regroups both historical Gaullists and the Christian Democrat centrists. It has a multi-ethnic basis, with around 20% of Kanak, 60% of Europeans, 80% of Polynesians and 80% of Asians. Its program focuses on economic development and access to education and health for everyone. The charter of the "Rassemblement" states that the "Melanesian promotion" and the land reform are a necessity.

In 1978, Jacques Lafleur is elected as representative of one of the two new districts in the first round with 55% of votes. The division, decided in Paris, allows the Caledonian Union to maintain a parliamentary seat in the second district. The Caledonian Union takes note of the electoral evolutions, its general secretary Jean-Marie Tjibaou stating: *"Twenty-five years ago, the motto «Two colours, one people " corresponded to an ethnic reality because only the two main groups, the blacks and the whites, were the essential elements of local politics. Neither the West Indians nor the Wallisians nor the Tahitians, nor Metropolitan nor Métis had such an important place as today.*

These new geographical data of local politics obliges us to reconsider the meaning of our motto which no longer fits perfectly with the ethnic reality of the territory. It must now be regarded as the symbol of our mutual commitment to dialogue".

Oral tradition - unconfirmed - is that François Mitterrand, then first secretary of the Socialist Party, has declared in 1978 to representative Rock Pidjot, that he supported the independence of New Caledonia. It is from this hypothetical promise that independence activists would have estimated that the time had come to strengthen their claims and develop their actions on the ground.

The fact that General Secretary of the UC, Pierre Declecq, announces in June 1979, for his party, that *«independence now passes first for us"* will have unintended consequences, as New Caledonians of all ideological tendencies join the RPCR in order to defend foremost New Caledonia within France. Thus, the very next day, Socialist Alain Bernut calls to vote for RPCR in the upcoming elections.

That same year, the majority of Kanak parties unite before the elections, in a pro--Independence Front. At the territorial election on July 1, 1979 the centrists of the FNSC progress with 7 seats, RPCR obtains 15 seats and the pro-Independence Front 14 seats. The agreement signed between the two anti-independence parties provides an alternative to the presidency of the Territorial Assembly, while the vice-presidency of the Government Council will remain with RPCR. Also, JP Aïfa

(FNSC) is reappointed as President of the Territorial Assembly, while RPCR and the Federation for a New Caledonian Society are sharing out the seven seats of government advisors, under the leadership of Loyaltian Dick Ukeiwé.

This new majority votes in January 1980 the beginning of a direct tax, a solidarity tax of 15% on the income exceeding 372 000 CFP per month. In June 1981, J. Lafleur is re-elected in the first round with 54% (16,289 votes) of the votes. His opponent Stanley Camerlynck (FNSC), obtains 5549 votes. In the second district, Rock Pidjot (UC, 6348 votes) expects to be elected in the second round before RPCR Henri Wetta (5252) and LKS Nidoish Naisseline (3517). Electoral equilibria are now clearly in favour of parties which promote the maintaining of New Caledonia within France.

New Caledonia enters a new period of decentralization and progress in autonomy, a period which is economically driven by the export of ore and nickel, metal which the archipelago is the third largest producer in the world. This resource is all the more important to the health of the local economy as the small size of New Caledonian population allows full employment and the implementation of real policies of redistribution.

Meanwhile, France participates more and more in the New Caledonia budget, the most symbolic example being the Caledonian Union vote in 1965 that gives to the State the management of secondary education, in order not to increase the local tax burden. Now, the state budget is greater than the territorial budget.

New Caledonia starts living on stilts that is to say beyond its means. This was soon criticized by economist Jean Fress who considers that the entry of New Caledonia in the consumer society may delay the process of independence for which he campaigned.

The election of the General Secretary of the Socialist Party, François Mitterrand, as President of the French Republic, in May 1981, accelerates the movement of claims and causes the

Kanak independence movement, which then represents only 30% of the population, to request for an immediate independence

However, François Mitterrand, once elected, considers the New Caledonian question differently. He wants himself to be the President of all the French and chooses to defend his conception of the highest interests of the nation. New Caledonia having 70% of non-independence voters, he decides to respect the democratic process. At the same time, the new national government unofficially supports the independence parties

The May 1981 elections, the left-right political divide of France matched the divide between pro-independence and anti-independence in the New Caledonian archipelago The anti-independence worry because if the fifty-eighth of the 110 proposals for France of the candidate François Mitterrand did not specifically evoke potential independence overseas (change, identity, rights to achieve their aspirations), and if his pre-electoral programme was as generous as imprecive (dialogue, identity, right to be oneself), the proposals in the government program signed in June 1972 with the French Communist Party and the promises of the socialist project in 1979, are still in the memories.

Since his appointment, the Secretary of State, Emmanuelli wants to appease by sending the following telegram to Jacques Lafleur: "Above all, the will expressed by the people to stay within the framework of the Republic will be taken into account, the links of solidarity will be preserved and strengthened". However, the new High Commissioner Christian Nucci favours independence parties and tries to create a new local majority, closer to the new national majority.

The assassination of the General Secretary of the UU, Pierre Declecq on September 19, 1981 provokes two days later, the first barricades and the interruption the Cyclist Tour of New Caledonia, some pro-independence consider that it is a political assassination. The case has never been solved, the separatists consider Pierre Declercq as a political martyr.

The High Commissioner is involved in the weakening of the RPCR (resignations of Frank Wahuzue and Marie-Paule Serve) and leads the FNSC to terminate on 15 June 1982 the agreement of government RPCR-FNSC in order to give, from1982 to 1984, the political majority to the Independence Front led by Jean-Marie Tjibaou. Their government contract is entitled "a government of civil peace, brotherhood and development."

Jacques Lafleur resigns on July 6, 1982 from his seat as MP in order to obtain new elections, in the pure Gaullist tradition. He is re-elected on September 5th 91 with.42% of the votes cast, which clearly means that the electorate of the FNSC separates, like in a U turn, from the general staff of the party.

On 6 January 1983 the "gendarmerie" in Touho is attacked by seventy separatists. Then, on January 10, during an operation of law enforcement to ensure the recovery of material from a sawmill, several shots are fired near La Foa. Two gendarmes are killed and six wounded when people respond with gunfire to the charge of the gendarmes. The Koindé syndrome explains the subsequent refusal of many high officials to advise authoritarian measures, paralyzed by the idea of another drama that can be attributed to them.

The municipal elections of March 1983 show that the political map of New Caledonia is more complex than just a battle between two opposing blocs: anti-independence and pro-independence. Noumea and Mont Dore will have two municipal councils fully RPCR. For the 30 other municipalities, 10 are acquired by the FI, 4 by the RPCR, 7 by elected without political labels and 9 by multi-ethnic groups united by communal management.

State Secretary George Lemoine brings together from 8 to 12 July 1983, in Nainville-les-roches, the major New Caledonian political components. The final declaration is accepted by the UC (other independence parties were absent) and the FNSC, but refused by the RPCR.. "1) - *Common will to see participants definitively confirm the abolition of colonialism by recognition of the equality of Melanesian culture and the manifestation of its representation by custom within institutions to be defined.*

2) - Recognition of the legitimacy of the Kanak people first occupant of the territory, to whom one recognize an innate and active right to independence, whose exercise must be accomplished in the context of self-determination provided and defined by the Constitution of the French Republic, self-determination also open, for historical reasons to other ethnic groups whose legitimacy is recognized by the representatives of the Kanak people.

3) - Promote the exercise of self-determination is "a French vocation» which must lead to a choice, including the right to independence. This approach of self-determination must be prepared and will be the fact of the Caledonian people as defined by the above admitted logic, and when it will feel this need. To prepare this approach, everyone is aware that we must develop a status of internal autonomy which will be specific, able to evolve and which will mark a transition taking into account political and economic data for there will be no economic development without political stability.

When Georges Lemoyne presents the new status in New Caledonia, not only RPCR boycotts his visit, but when presenting the project to the Territorial Assembly neither RPCR nor Independence Front are present.

* "Years of ashes" 1984 -1988.

During the territorial elections of November 18, 1984, despite the announcement of an active boycott by the FI and the symbolic destruction of an ballot box by Eloi Machoro, with an axe, in Canala, participation is 57.5%. RPCR alone gets 27,851 votes or 70.87% of the vote. So RPCR obtain the majority of seats that is to say 34 seats out of 42.

Dick Ukeiwé is elected as President of the Government by 35 votes; the RPCR is obliged to note the favourable FN vote, while regretting the choice of JP Aïfa (ULO) to abstain. The government of this loyalist Loyaltian includes nine ministers, four of whom are Melanesians.

Following these elections, the National Liberation Kanak and Socialist Front, which replaced the FI, a step further in activism, leaving its supporters multiply land occupations in the 'bush', investing gendarmeries, by drawing barricades and taking hostages. Judge François Seymur lists 1,800 violent actions (including 257 arsons and 950 thefts of possessions or weapons).

On 5 December 1984, a group of seven mixed-race loyalists in Hienghène, infuriated by the violent actions of FLNKS intercept two vehicles and kill ten pro-independence Melanesians, including two brothers of Jean-Marie Tjibaou. Premeditation is proven and emotion is great for both sides, because if warmongers approve this act of "war", the silent majority condemns this barbaric act and the separatist actions that made it possible. The repercussion is the assassination of the loyalist Jean-Marie Sangarne, in Hienghène, on December 10.

On January 11, 1985 the murder of Yves Tual, a young bushman shot in the head, on the family property, causes violent anti-independence demonstrations in Noumea. At this moment the President of the Republic agreed to the neutralization operation of Eloi Machoro, independence leader responsible for the occupation of Thio, rushing to the west coast at the head of thirty five armed FLNKS militants. A group of Special Forces (GIGN) is specially sent from France for this operation. On the order of Edgard Pisani, Jean-Pierre Picon and his elite gendarmes make customary warning before firing: Eloi Machoro and his lieutenant Marcel Nonnaro are then mortally wounded.

The Fabius-Pisani status is promulgated on August 23 1985. In local elections on 29 September 1985 the new districting allows separatists to manage three of the four new regions. In contrast, the RPCR maintains its majority in the Congrès of the Territory that includes the elected representatives from the four regions, the South region, much more populated, (85 000 or 60%) including 45% of the seats

Therefore, the loyalists are eagerly awaiting the general elections, considering that it will bring alternation and a different future. Indeed, on 16 March 1986, the national majority is changed, involving the establishment of the first "cohabitation". The policy of the new national government is inspired by the principle of republican equality:" a man, one vote", which means that the will of the majority should be applied, since it is that of democracy. It does not take into account the specific history of New Caledonia and condemns the pro-independence Kanak to remain permanently in opposition.

In New Caledonia, Jacques Lafleur is re-elected on March 16, 1986, the second seat, for the first time, is also attributed to the RPCR (Maurice Nénou), due to the slowdown of FLNKS.

Economically, the separatists, despite their former hawkish speeches, carefully manage the three regions they chair. Upon his appointment as minister of overseas territories, Bernard Pons starts working on a new status that corresponds to the wishes of the local majority. It is promulgated on January 22 1988. In the meantime, he publishes the law of 17 July 1986 providing for a self-determination referendum in September 1987. Without consultation with the separatists, the question is changed. It is no longer about independence-association, but it becomes, *"Do you want that New Caledonia becomes independent or remains within the French Republic? »*

It is decided that all voters residing for at least three years in the country will participate in the elections. The national government has locked and changed the meaning of the referendum. Participation is only 59%, following the instruction of an active boycott of voting, the "yes" to France getting 98% of the votes.

When Bernard Pons announced on 26 January 1988 that local New Caledonian elections and the first round of the presidential election will be held the same day, April 24, the tone rises. Indeed, the separatists do not like the new regional divisions established, since they are not sure to head three of the four regions. Similarly, the changes in the new status return the main previous autonomist advances to the Jacobin state

Jean-Marie Tjibaou does not exclude that Kanak could return to armed action: *"For Kanak today, we can only discuss with weapons in hand. »* He therefore orders the actively boycott of April elections and calls the basic units to" *organize resistance by all means"*. The first test, visible by all, of this new FLNKS direction, is the taking of hostages in Tiéti, an area in the municipality of Poindimié.

On April 14, Tjibaou wrote his letter to the President and candidate François Mitterrand: *"Mr. President, what future are you preparing for us? Shall we be the last of the Mohicans of the Pacific region, as there was the last Tasmanians? You know it, the Kanak People has always refused to be considered as an archaeological relic of the world history. It will even more refuse to be that of the French colonial history ... When Mr. Pons, after stating that the FLNKS was only a small group, sends twenty-nine additional squadrons of riot police for the elections of 24 April (bringing the number of armed men to eleven thousand for seventy-five thousand men, women and Kanak children), Why is this ? "*

François Mitterrand integrates its response to his "Letter to the French" that recognizes the existence of two legitimacies and advises good relationship.

* The Ouvea drama (April 22-May 5, 1988)

An ordinary morning in Ouvea, April 22 1988, hoisting of colours in the gendarmerie of Fayaoué. The 31 policemen, three "territorial" and 28 mobile, came as reinforcements for the elections, begin an uneventful day in "the island closest to paradise."

Chanel Kapoeri, FLNKS regional councillor and vice-president of the Loyalty Islands region, enters the gendarmerie. First he discusses with the Melanesian gendarme Samuel Ihage, before going to the office of brigadier. Some banalities are exchanged and then the four visitors remove knives and tomahawks from of their clothes. Chanel Kapoeri screams: "You are our prisoners! »

Four gendarms die in minutes. Others are then gathered in the centre of the court and the armoury is emptied of its content. Around 9 am, the gendarmes, handcuffed, come out of the brigade in army vehicles. A group of eleven hostages head south. Two days later, Chanel Kapoeri, who has had time to think about the consequences of the hostage-taking and has no blood of the dead policemen on his conscience, leads his men to accept full and complete surrender.

The northern group leave in three 4x4, two jeeps and a Land Rover and take refuge in a sacred cave. As soon as the news of the hostage-taking arrived in Noumea, 270 gendarmes go to Ouvea. The airfield of Ouloup is immediately secured by the "soldiers of the law."

We are in the context of the presidential election. All decisions are estimated for their influence on the French public opinion, not based on ground realities.

In negotiations, both parties must be willing to discuss and to compromise. The State can not be lax because four gendarmes died: the kidnappers must surrender and go to jail. Alphonse Dianou expresses unacceptable claims.

Captain Philippe Legorjus tries - unsuccessfully - to get the FLNKS to break the deadlock. It makes sense that Jean-Marie Tjibaou and the Political Bureau of the FLNKS have remained silent throughout the hostage crisis. Any response would have driven, in the short or medium term, to a very high probability of deterioration of the situation, until a real civil war ensues

Finally, the highest authorities of the State order to free the hostages. On May 5, the Victor operation is a human achievement since all the hostages are delivered. But it is also a failure since two soldiers and nineteen pro-independence militants are killed, including the head of the kidnappers, Alphonse Dianou. Similarly, if the Victor operation is successful tactically and militarily, it is a failure in the medias because the army has not been able to manage the rights of press on national soil, while blunders were a much better journalistic topic - whatever the cost - than maintaining public order.

Paradoxically, the Ouvea case has avoided civil war. New Caledonia had been so close to it that all political actors made the effort to resume dialogue and find a negotiated solution acceptable to all parties. The death of Jean-Marie Tjibaou is a direct consequence of his pragmatic and responsible management of the Ouvea drama. His unacceptable death had the immediate effect to permanently wipe out the radical separatists and, as a back on effect, to engrave on marble the Matignon-Oudinot Agreements that enabled economic prosperity and peace to flourish again.

The Ouvea case is therefore one of the key events that allowed the peaceful development of the recent history of New Caledonia. This collective tragedy has forced both parties to real introspection, coupled with a Cornelian dilemma: civil peace around a minimal accord or civil war accompanied by new processions of dead and tears.

Michel Rocard's bet on intelligence, embodied in the famous hand shake of Jean-Marie Tjibaou and Jacques Lafleur is the direct result of the dead in Ouvea, whether they are police, Kanaks or GIGN, victims or kidnappers, assassinated or murdered, or executed. Ouvea was the trigger for the expected peace, the possible peace and finally the found peace.

Chapter VI.
From Accords to contemporary New Caledonia

The Matignon-Oudinot Accords, then the Noumea Accords, confer a new status to New Caledonia, which is no longer an overseas territory but becomes a specific French community, while waiting to become a single entity endowed with a progressively extended autonomy, increasing powers transferred from State to New Caledonia.

* The period of the 1988-1998 Accords.
The hostages-taking in Ouvéa made the French State, FLNKS and RPCR aware that New Caledonia was likely to fall at any time into civil war. Michel Rocard, Jean-Marie Tjibaou and Jacques Lafleur are aware that the saying "never again" must prevail. After the Ouvea massacre, Tjibaou wonders if "One does not hurt the people with only slogans." Jacques Lafleur maintains the need for power sharing and economic wealth. This dual awareness of the need to reverse the history mechanism, allows the signing of the Matignon Accords. Michel Rocard will comment on the June 26 accord as follows: *«Both delegations have accepted the urgent need to contribute to restore civil peace in order to create the conditions in which the populations will be able to choose, freely and assured of their future, the mastery of their fate."*
On May 5, 1988, François Mitterrand was re-elected as President. In terms of local elections, the RPCR win 35 seats, on its right the "Front National" get 8 seats, the "Caledonian Front" 2 seats and 1 seat goes to the "l'Entente" list, while the only separatist list of Francis Pabouty " Unir pour Construire" (United To Build) win 1 seat.
The new Prime Minister Michel Rocard impulses a new policy. He sends to Nouméa, on 20 May 1988, the dialogue mission whose first goal is to allow the resumption of normal relations; after the lasting and major trauma of the Ouvea

troubles. Indeed, no way out is possible if the antagonistic sides lock themselves in their resentment.

Thanks to the general good will, the Matignon Accords were signed on June 26 1988 It is a minimum agreement as shown in the final press release. This framework agreement provides that the Territory will be directly administered by the State for a year, before putting up a new statute establishing three Provinces, and a self-determination vote that will take place in 1998. In New Caledonia, reservations are strong.

The second round of talks was finalized August 20, 1988 when Dick Ukeiwé, heading RPCR delegation and Jean-Marie Tjibaou sign the Oudinot Accords, whose short-term goal is to restructure the New Caledonian political life (15 statutes in 32 years), its long-term goal being the economic, social and cultural balance of the Territory. It specifically mentions a necessary balance between the Kanak and other communities, between Noumea and the rest of the archipelago and finally, between the three provinces that have just been created. A self-determination vote is expected in 1998.

The new statute, said Rocard status, is endorsed by referendum Nov. 6, 1988, all French voters to vote on the following question: *" Do you approve the draft law submitted to the French people by the President of the Republic on statutory provisions and preparatory to self-determination of New Caledonia in 1998 "*

Officially, the referendum method is applied in order to give legitimacy to the process put in place. In fact, it is used primarily to allow the freezing of the electorate for the final referendum to *"people interested in the future of New Caledonia"* (Article 2), that is to say, the Kanaks, the "victims of history" (transported settlers, engaged, polynesian immigrants) and all french citizens who arrived before 1988, as well as amnesty for crimes (articles. 80) "political, economic and social order." Indeed, these items could have been censored by the Conseil d'Etat for a simple bill. Consulting shows a high rate of abstention and if the "Yes" far outweighs nationally by 80%, it is barely a majority in Caledonia, with 57% of votes.

During their visit to Ouvea on May 4, 1989, to witness the ending of customary mourning period for the deceded of the Gossanah cave, Jean-Marie Tjibaou and his sidekick Yeiwéné Yeiwéné are murdered by Djubelly Wea. The latter was killed by Jean-Michel Tjibaou's bodyguard a native of Hienghène, just like him.

The Prime Minister traveled to Noumea for the funeral of the two separatist leaders. Their coffins were draped with the Kanaky flag "officialised" by Jean-Marie Tjibaou in November 1984. The Tjibaou myth can begin to grow and develop.

François Burck, former New Caledonian priest, like Jean-Marie, becomes president of the Caledonian Union. The following year, the former chief of staff of Jean-Marie Tjibaou, Paul Néaoutyine, becomes president of FLNKS. Á the same time, keeping his promise to Jean-Marie Tjibaou, Jacques Lafleur sells his shares in the Mining Company of the South Pacific to the Northern Province for 1.8 billion CFP francs, the necessary capital being compensated by the State.

Law No. 88-1028 of November 9, 1988 sets up the Rocard status, that must be applied from 12 July 1989. New Caledonia is now divided into three Provinces. In addition, for purposes of "social peace" the new status recognizes the Melanesian specificity through the Customary Advisory Council, the Agency for the Development of the "Canaque" Culture (then Kanak) or the start of the construction of the JM Tjibaou Cultural Centre, which is one of the major projects of the presidency of the French Republic. Designed by architect Renzo Piano, it includes ten huts combining contemporary and traditional materials and is finally inaugurated on 4 May 1998.

Meanwhile, the balance in favour of the Melanesian world is also based on development contracts between the State and the Provinces, on the construction of the Koné-Tiwaka road, on the " 400 graduates Programme", aiming to train New

Caledonians (mainly of Melanesian origin) aver a 10 year period, and the transfer of the "Agency for Rural Development and Land Development Planning", from the Territory to the State. The ADRAF distributes 82,000 ha between 1989 and 1995, allowing a 36% increase in the Melanesian land area.

Factually, the different elections allow a majority to the RPCR in the Southern Province and in Congress, separatists having the majority in the North and Islands provinces. In the first Provincial elections, on June 11, 1989, Jacques Lafleur wins the presidency of the Southern Province, Leopold Jorédié the presidency of the Northern Province and Richard Kaloí the presidency the Loyalty Islands Province.

In 1995, the second term of the Matignon Agreements confirms the forces involved in the political situation, with a variant. The presidency of the Loyalty Islands Province is no longer provided by the Caledonian Union, but by the president of LKS, Nidoish Naisseline, through its alliance with the RPCR and a party coming from the UC: the FDIL.

The RPCR, with its experience of years of ash and its mission to be a force for political union gives prominence to Melanesians. Thus Dick Ukeiwé becomes a European Representative in June 1988 and Simon Louekhote is elected, the same month, president of the Congrès of New Caledonia. In 1992, he becomes the youngest Senator of France.

On April 27, 1991, at an RPCR convention, its president Jacques Lafleur launches the idea of a "consensual solution" to avoid a cleaver referendum that would inevitably be won by supporters of the maintaining in the French Republic (65% of voters), but that probably would have the side-effect of an uprange of violence. The main pro-independence party, the Caledonian Union takes up the idea at its convention in Paita in 1993, preferring the designation of "negotiated independence."

The negotiations are soon parasitized by the issue of access to the mineral resource, SMSP wishing to exchange a mining perimeter with SLN-Eramet in order to have sufficient resources for the establishment of a metallurgical project with the Canadian company Falconbridge. This important «precondition" is finally settled by the State during the Bercy Accords favouring the interests of the Northern Province.

* The Noumea Accords, contrition and evolutionary status
In the preamble of the Noumea Accords, France, by "a strong gesture," recognizes the "lights and shadows" of the colonial period and the trauma suffered by Kanaks, while paying tribute to the different communities who participated in the construction of New Caledonia.

Extract of the preamble :*"1. When France takes possession of La Grande Terre, that James Cook had named "New Caledonia" on September 24, 1853, it takes a territory under the terms of international law then recognized by the nations of Europe and America, but it does not establish legal relations with the native population. Treaties signed with the customary authorities are not balanced agreements but, in fact, unilateral acts. However, this territory was not empty.*

La Grande Terre and the Islands were inhabited by men and women who were named Kanak. They had developed their own civilization, with its traditions, languages, custom governing the social and political field. Their culture and psychological universe were expressed in various forms of creativity.

They had developed their own civilization, with its traditions, languages, custom governing the social and political field. Their culture and psychological universe were expressed in various forms of creativity. The Kanak identity was based on a special relationship to the land. Each individual, each clan was defined by a specific link to a valley, a hill, the sea, a river mouth, and kept the other families host memory. The names that tradition gave to each element of the landscape, taboos marking some of them, customary paths were organizing space and exchanges.

2 The colonization of New Caledonia was part of a broader historical movement in which European countries have imposed their domination to the world.

Men and women came in large numbers, in the nineteenth and twentieth centuries, convinced to bring progress, driven by their religious faith, came against their will or seeking a second chance in New Caledonia. They settled there and they established a line. They brought with them their ideals, their knowledge, their hopes, their ambitions, their illusions and contradictions.

Among them some, especially men of culture, priests and pastors, doctors and engineers, administrators, soldiers, politicians looked differently at the original people, with a greater understanding or genuine compassion. New populations in the territory participated, in often difficult conditions, providing scientific and technical knowledge, to the development of mining and agriculture and, with the help of the State, to the development of New Caledonia. Their determination and inventiveness have laid the foundations for development...

3 It is time to recognize the shadows of the colonial period, though it was not devoid of light. The impact of colonization was a lasting trauma for the original population...

4 Decolonization is a way to rebuild a lasting social link between communities now living in New Caledonia, allowing the Kanak people to establish with France, new relationships according to the realities of our time...,

Today it is necessary to lay the foundations of a citizenship for New Caledonia, allowing the original people to build, with men and women who live here, a human community asserting its common destiny...

The past was the time of colonization. This is the time of sharing, through rebalancing. The future must be the time of identity in a common destiny.... "

After a period of twenty years, in 2018, a referendum is planned, in which a limited electorate will decide on a possible total emancipation, that is to say, a political independence.

The autonomy granted to the provinces by the Matignon Accords is also recognized for the benefit of New Caledonia, which has a collegial government in charge of the executive while Congrès enacts the "laws of the country." Customary Senate, composed of representatives of the eight customary areas, must be consulted for all matters relating to the Kanak identity. Finally, emerges a "citizenship of New Caledonia' which leads to the establishment of a restricted electorate for the elections of the members of Provincial Assemblies, for referendums on self-determination, and the notion of priority on local employment.

Rendered applicable by a revision of the constitution passed by the Parliament on 20 July 1998, the Noumea Accords are ratified by the referendum of 8 November 1998 where 'yes' wins much more clearly on the 'no' by comparison with the referendum of 1988. The text of the Accords is likely to have three different readings: full internal autonomy, full independence, or emancipation within the French Republic

* Perpetuation of the bipolarization of politics (1998-2004)

The first elections confirm the large majority of the RPCR of Jacques Lafleur. The party leads in fact the Southern Province, the Congrès of New Caledonia (local legislature), the Government of New Caledonia (local executive), the Economic and Social Council, the majority of urban and suburban communities (Noumea, Mont -Dore, Paita, La Foa, and since 2001, Bourail). Accordingly, the party controls the Chambers of Commerce, the Administration and the territorial Publics Offices.

FLNKS manage the Northern Province (Palika) and The Islands (UC and Palika), most small rural communities and Customary Senate. FLNKS has a veto power in the collegial government of New Caledonia, and elected representatives in all local elected powers.

It must be noted that the parity law requires political parties to widely accept women in municipal councils in 2001 and obliges them to list equally male and female candidates for the provincial election of 2004.

Since January 2000, the transfer of competences began under the presidency of Jean Lèques' government, and then of Pierre Frogier, unhurriedly, as each transfer involves the full examination of the administrative sector concerned and the establishment, by agreement State-Country, of a budget equivalent to expenditures induced by any new responsibility. In 2003, during the one hundred and fiftieth anniversary of the annexation by France, communities gather around the Mwakaa (home of humanity) in the centre of Noumea. September 24 commemorate citizenship.

The energy of the main political parties turned to the major economic development projects. Indeed, RPCR wants to ensure economic growth and FLNKS wants to build the country. Each province sets its economic priorities based on its political orientations. Province Islands favour spatial planning, ecotourism, and support to commercial crops compatible with traditional social organization. Northern Province sets four goals: a real economic boom, internal balance between the both coasts, establishment of private companies for job creation and environmental protection. Southern Province, where population pressure increases, opts for social housing, youth integration and economic development.

Land of contrasts, New Caledonia is a land of socio-economic disparities. Thus, in 2002, among 210 000 people, 135 000 reside in the Southern Province and only 23,000 in the Loyalty Islands. The population of the Northern Province and the Islands Province is made up of mainly of Melanesians (97 and 80%), while the Southern Province has 75% non-Kanak. Meanwhile, 88% of salaried jobs are in the south, while the

Islands Province generates only 2%. Finally, if Noumea then has 80 000 inhabitants, the nearby dormitory towns have only 20,000 (Mont-Dore), 14000 (Dumbéa) and 8000 (Paita). Each of the first three towns in the "'bush" totalize only about 4,500 inhabitants: Bourail, Poindimié and Houaïlou

The strengths of the economy outweigh: stability of institutions; mineral reserves of at least 25% of world nickel; an under-utilized Exclusive Economic Zone; rare infrastructures in Oceania islands; a high level of training; multiple development aid; a high standard of living, made possible in part by large transfers from France, low inflation; fauna and flora largely endemic; the largest closed lagoon in the world; agriculture relatively protected by insularity. The range of training courses is increasingly diverse. Thus the French University of the Pacific opens in 1987 in Magenta. This State University, now become University of New Caledonia in 1999, was created to help Oceanian students of low-income families. The premature death of its first president, Paul de Deckker, delayed its integration in the South Pacific. Under his authority and that of Professor Jean-Yves Faberon, over one hundred Kanaks and Caledonians of European origin obtained DEA, Masters and PhD theses, both in Humanities and in Law.

By contrast, New Caledonia suffers from: the decline in its air service, the small size of its domestic market, the multiplication of administrative skills, customs protection, unsufficient knowledge of the dominant language at the regional level, important cost of work and a certain politicization of economic life. Indeed, for some economists, "the politicization of everything has pernicious economic effects. To invest locally often involves to be appreciated by those who control the political power. "

Nevertheless, the economic future of New Caledonia is already based in the eventual implementation of the three mining projects competing against each other. At the same time, without much media coverage, Société Le Nickel

(Doniambo, Eramet-SLN) increases in 2005 the annual production of the smelter in Noumea from 60 000 to 75 000 tonnes of nickel-metal.

In the early twenty-first century, the health of the New Caledonian economy is satisfactory, the main problem remains the difficulty of providing enough jobs annually to new contingent of young adults entering the labour market. This explains the importance given by both the New Caledonian government and the various unions, to the issue of local employment. And in fact, some politicians say that the debate on independence is no longer the real issue, considering that the real challenge of the future will be access or not of all New Caledonians to employment.

* Redistribution of political order in 2004

In the 2004 elections, the historic partners of the Matignon and Noumea Accords cannot overcome their internal divisions: the RPCR splits into two parts of equal size; FLNKS is unable to present combined lists. After the 2004 elections, the "Rassemblement" (UMP) loses the three most important presidencies.

First, through an agreement with the" National Front", the" Future Together" obtained the presidency of the Southern Province for Philippe Gomès. Second, the "Rassemblement" loses the presidency of the Congress, that it held since 1989, in favour of Harold Martin, candidate of "Future Together" elected in the second round with the votes of pro-Independence of UC and LKS, and those of the National Front. Third, June 10, 2004, the new collegial Government of the Territory is elected, headed by two women, Marie-Noëlle Thémereau ("Future Together", president) and Déwé Gorodey (Palika, vice president).

Following an internal disagreement within "Future Together", the two seats of representatives are kept by the "Rassemblement-UMP". The big loser of this general elections is Jacques Lafleur, beaten by his substitute.

Soon after, Pierre Frogier leads "Future Together" to abandon most of the ideas advocated by Philippe Gomès, in order to accept, on 30 July 2008, a framework agreement with the majority "Rassemblement-UMP". Harold Martin becomes, in August 2008, President of the Government and Pierre Frogier takes the seat of President of Congrès. The internal fracture that was created during the general elections obliges Philippe Gomès to quit the party that had defeated Jacques Lafleur in 2004 in order to found, in November 2008, "Caledonia Together".

The issue of identity signs progresses at the end of the mandate. The collegial Government adopts, on June 26, 2008, during a special session, a draft "law of the country" endorsing the choice of an anthem and a motto, and the new design of banknotes. The chosen motto is "Land of speech, sharing land" while the hymn entitled "Let us be united, let us become brothers" urges communities of the archipelago to concord.

New Caledonia accounts according to the 2008 census, reappraised like all censuses by some political parties, 245,580 people and 135,964 voters eligible to vote in provincial elections (87.6% of the electorate). 18,208 other voters of French nationality not meeting the criteria of the Noumea Accords cannot vote. The main political issue in this election concerns the Noumea Agreements: should it apply, how and for what institutional changes?

Election results generally recognize the reality of the two blocks involved, the anti-independence representing 60% of voters and 85% of people in the South Province, while the separatists probably correspond to 80% of Melanesian voters, which assure them of the government of the two other provinces. The return of pro-independence representatives in the Southern province is hailed by all and the disappearance of any anti-independence representative in the Loyalty Islands is perceived by all as a loss in terms of democracy.

The Rassemblement-UMP comes first with 28.5% of the votes, leading the historian Luc Steinmetz to consider that it found «not a dominant but prominent position." It appears that the two parties resulting from "Future Together" rose by 23% and their combined voices are higher than those of the "Rassemblement-UMP".

In the independence sphere of influence, appears the successful breakthrough of the Labour Party, political offshoot of USTKE close to the French ultra-left union. Despite 2,227 votes (3%) in the Southern Province, no representative is elected, but some are in the North and Islands provinces. In the following months, the party approaches the Caledonian Union.

Pierre Frogier, President of the "Rassemblement-UMP", is the first to propose on May 12, 2009 *a distribution of the institutional responsibilities based on the proportional representation."* This "republican rally", initiated by the "Rassemblement-UMP", sets up a triple alliance between "Rassemblement", "Caledonia Together" and "Future Together".

Pierre Frogier, a "Rassemblement-UMP" representative, becomes the third president of the Southern Province. Philippe Gomes, president of "Caledonia Together", becomes chief of executive of New Caledonia. The Leader of "Future Together", Harold Martin, accepts the presidency of the Congrès.

On the economic front, the progressive construction of two smelters in the North (Vavouto with Swiss Glencore) and South (Goro with Brazilian Vale) provides employment for the majority of unskilled job seekers, and during several years. The "law of the country" on local employment is in line with the necessary new balance, so that all Caledonians fully access to monetary or urban economy, and to globalization, if they so desire. Training, especially technical education, is at the centre of all strategies to improve the daily lives of all New Caledonians.

The infrastructure of the country, long overdue, is now closer to European standards and superior to those of independent

States islands of Pacific. Moreover, local Red Cross and the Armed Forces based in New Caledonia fully participate, together with Australia and New Zealand, to regional humanitarian actions. Presumably under the institutional changes, if Noumea leaves the Noumea Accords, the regalian authority, represented by Foreign Affairs, will be increasingly shared.

Public expenditure (not the budget that is reductive) in New Caledonia is roughly made up of:
- 25% direct and indirect taxes on households
- 50% direct and indirect transfers of the France
- 25% mine and metallurgy sector, knowing that many tax exemptions are reducing the cost of three multinational operators exploiting Caledonian nickel. So some observers believe that New Caledonia, as long as France continues to support it, could access to political independence.

On the one hand, one might think that France would reduce drastically its support to a new country, as evidenced by the example of Vanuatu, the former Franco-British condominium of New Hebrides. On the other hand, the reduction in government expenditure would lead to the disappearance of a number of positions in public services and the reduction of the salaries of remaining employees hence the fall in direct taxes. Reduction of the New Caledonian civil service, representing more than 10% of the working population, would involve a drop in consumption, and cause the reduction of indirect taxes. Furthermore, there is no evidence that the taxation of the mining sector would continue to provide significant resources, especially when the mineral resources sector is undergoing substantial fluctuations and serrated changes.

François Guard rightly says: *"The problem of the independence of New Caledonia will be ended with the independence of New Caledonia."* This does not mean that there is any meaning in history, but that the debate on independence must remain institutional, as long as its supporters represent a significant political force. So New Caledonia will have a choice in the coming decades, between a progressive solution reached by consensus inside in the French block and an independence that will involve at least an important change in the way of life of all New Caledonians.

Á dawn of the 2010s, the main concern of the unions - New Caledonia is one of the few countries to know almost full employment - is the cost of living. Indeed, the fact that the New Caledonian population is less than 300,000 inhabitants puts a number of issues (employment, crime, political conflicts) into perspective. At the same time, the small size of the market partially explains prices increased by 40% (vehicles, books) to 200% (many food products). The importance of indirect taxation, the turn of margins in the world of import and freight costs, also affect prices. Now all the Caledonians want to integrate into the consumer society. In this regard, the example of squats, that is to say, spontaneous dwellings on land left fallow by public or private owners, is significant. Some correspond to real poverty. Others are the first stage of rural exodus and include some modern consumer goods, while their occupants have quality cars.

Culturally, local authorities are increasingly concerned about the cultural heritage with the opening in 2014 of a museum of the American presence, in a genuine "half-moon" and a museum of the prison at Nou Island. Each province has its listed monuments and sites, or its movable heritage (ancient sculptures, altars, guillotine, grinders, locomotives), while bringing much attention to the protection of natural areas. The Caledonian lagoon is, however, listed as World Heritage by UNESCO in 2008. The local government has created a Society of Authors, Composer and Editors of New Caledonia and a status of casual workers in Arts and Humanities is being drafted.

* A second "bet on intelligence"

The proposal issued on February 10, 2010 by the President of the Rassemblement-UMP to implement reflection able to lead to fly the FLNKS flag ("free of struggles"), alongside the French tricolor, renews the political debate, on both identifying symbols and reflections about the end of the Noumea Accords. This outstretched hand proves to be a particularly strong act, because its initiator asks for nothing in return.

According to Pierre Frogier, the pro-independence have made a significant gesture by accepting the legitimacy of newcomers in 1988. The State has made a similar gesture by adopting, together with the preamble of the Noumea Agreements, "an act of contrition" in 1998.

The anti-independence made, in 2010, a gesture of equal importance by accepting the symbol of Kanak nationalist struggle.

This announcement changes the political landscape as it is very positively received by the other main historical partner of the Agreements, the Caledonian Union. Palika, a component of FLNKS, accepts this token of political goodwill, while minimizing it. Future Together, which had already moved closer to Rassemblement-UMP, accepts it as a necessary element in the development of trusting relationships between people who work at the possible futures of New Caledonia.

The Caledonia Together party, which considers itself increasingly marginalized in the context of republican reconciliation and wants to return to action with the anti-independence voters, chose to violently reject "the two flags".

The institutional crisis took shape when the mayors of Caledonia Together refused to raise the Kanak identity nationalist flag. Caledonian Union, who also had internal problems to solve, resigned on February 17, 2011 the local government, which made it fall. At the new election, in proportion to the main Caledonian parties, Caledonia Together indicates that its elected representatives will immediately resign their election, to cause blockage of the institutions, in order to cause early general elections.

The Harold Martin government takes office on March 3, 2011 and immediately the elected of Caledonia Together resign. The State, in accordance with the political majority of the time, amends section 121 of the Caledonian organic law, to avoid the crisis to continue or to recur.

This analysis is not accepted by the majority of the New Caledonian electorate that is concerned in 2012 and that elects two Caledonia Together representatives: Philippe Gomes and Sonia Lagarde. Pierre Frogier makes the choice to resign from the Presidency of the Southern province, and Cynthia Ligeard becomes its fourth President. Former Rassemblement-UMP representative in the first district, Gaël Yanno creates, on July 27, 2013, his own party, the Caledonian Popular Movement.

Municipal and provincial elections in 2014 confim the new leadership of Caledonia Together. That party made an agreement with Rassemblement-UMP in 2017 to share the two nationals senators. Then the Caledonia Together party won the national deputies elections. Nearly all the non-independantist parties join together in a political "platform" to began to prepare the referendum on the future statute of New Caledonia in October 2018.

We refuse to comment on the recent events, due to the fact that we are neither in history nor in the history of the present, but in the time of the political controversy that all Caledonians are fearing, with their feelings and resentments. Let us not forget that electors often vote for a program, and also against the idea they have of a politician. And in politics, since ancient times, "there is not far from the Capitol to the Tarpeian Rock." Also, universal suffrage, if it is often predictable, opens the door to all the possibilities and all developments.

Conclusion

The Caledonian political landscape, since the tragedy in Ouvea and the original construction that followed, appears both changeless and changing. Thus, since the end of the political events, already more than two decades ago, every election gives 60% anti-independence and 40% of voters in favour of a new sovereignty. Similarly, the independence electorate represents about 75% of voters in the North and Islands province and 15% in the southern province.

At the same time, the political landscape is no longer composed of two monolithic blocks. Thus no party is now able to have a stable majority, even assisted by the second or the third party in terms of seats. Now, the old 1984-1988 demons clashes are floored and all alliances are possible and legitimate in order to build a better and more informed "country», which can marry the confines of the autonomy proposed by Le Rassemblement-UMP and an independence-association desired by FLNKS

Today, all the elements of a peaceful construction of New Caledonia's future are gathered. The defenders of maintaining New Caledonia in the Republic are willing to accept to go, with their separatist colleagues, up to the confines of autonomy. Forty percent of the Caledonians in favour of independence, that is to say seventy-five percent of Kanaks, are willing to respect the democratic process and the concept of "one man, one vote". In this respect, they obtained - so that immigration is no longer a politician issue - that the electorate concerned by the future provincial elections and referendums, corresponds to the definition of the "frozen electorate" as defined by the State in 2003. This specific electorate proving to be very exclusive and frozen on New Caledonia of 1990s, one might think that it will change in the future - after consultation between the state, FLNKS and anti-independence.

At the same time, nobody is able to say with certainty what the future of New Caledonia will be. The State can, at any time, modify its analysis of overseas issues. Separatists and supporters of keeping New Caledonia in the Republic are - as everywhere in the world –often caught in fratricidal struggles for valid reasons. Also, the input or output of the political spectrum of a single important elected representative can lead to significant changes regarding the equilibria involved. In a country which only 300,000 inhabitants, this means that all electoral evolutions are possible, even if it is logical to expect that common reason will prevail.

All are ready to participate in the construction of the common hut.
All consider their architectural model is the best.
All want to build the common future, which some prefer to call the common destiny.

Apart from politics, it appears that nickel ore remains at the heart of the economic and political future of New Caledonia. At the global level, the fact that the Caledonian "Caillou" contains 25 to 30% of world reserves, the relatively optimistic perception of New Caledonia's political realities and a suitable metallurgical market for at least a decade, allow international mining companies to invest locally billions of dollars.

Table of contents

Introduction

The Pacific battalion and the First World War
A dual society
A third of the population is Asian
The beneficial impact of Second World War
Contrasted results of colonization

**Part three
Present day,
From autonomy to decolonization, inside the French
political organization**

Chapter V. An original colonization (1945-1988)
Towards greater autonomy (1945-1958)
The apogee and decline of autonomy (1858-1974)
 Revival kanak and claims for independence (1975-1984)
The "years of ash", 1984-1988
The Ouvea drama (April 22-May 5, 1988)

**Chapter VI.   From Accords to contemporary New
Caledonia**
Time Accords, 1988-1998
The Noumea Accords, contrition and evolutionary status
Perpetuating the bipolarization of politics (1998-2004)
Redistribution of the political situation in 2004
A second "bet on intelligence"

Conclusion

www.ingramcontent.com/pod-product-compliance
Lightning Source LLC
Chambersburg PA
CBHW031248280526
45784CB00004B/1762